megan's secrets

megan's secrets

WHAT MY MENTALLY DISABLED DAUGHTER

TAUGHT ME ABOUT LIFE

MIKE COPE

LEAFWOOD
PUBLISHERS

MEGAN'S SECRETS
WHAT MY MENTALLY DISABLED DAUGHTER TAUGHT ME ABOUT LIFE

LEAFWOOD
P U B L I S H E R S

Copyright 2011 by Mike Cope

ISBN 978-0-89112-286-9
LCCN 2011008555

Printed in the United States of America

Scripture quotations, unless otherwise noted, are from The Holy Bible,
Today's New NIV. Copyright 2005, International Bible Society.
Used by permission of Zondervan Publishers.

"Welcome to Holland," by Emily Perl Kingsley. ©1987 by Emily Perl Kingsley. All rights
reserved. Reprinted by permission of the author. *Disappointment with God* by Philip Yancey.
© 1988 by Philip Yancey. Used by permission of Zondervan, www.zondervan.com. "On
the Death of the Beloved," from TO BLESS THE SPACE BETWEEN US: A BOOK OF BLESSINGS
by John O'Donohue. Copyright @ 2008 by John O'Donohue. Used by permission of
Doubleday, a division of Random House, Inc.

LIBRARY OF CONGRESS CATALOGING-IN-PUBLICATION DATA
Cope, Mike.
 Megan's secrets : what my mentally handicapped daughter taught me about life / Mike
Cope.
   p. cm.
 ISBN 978-0-89112-286-9
 1. Christian life--Churches of Christ authors. 2. Cope, Megan Diane, 1984-1994. 3. Mental
retardation--Religious aspects--Christianity. I. Title.
 BV4509.5.C673 2011
 248.8'66--dc22

                                                                              2011008555

Cover design by Thinkpen Design, LLC
Interior text design by Sandy Armstrong

Leafwood Publishers | 1626 Campus Court | Abilene, Texas 79601
1-877-816-4455 toll free

For current information about all Leafwood titles, visit our Web site:
www.leafwoodpublishers.com

                11 12 13 14 15 16 / 6 5 4 3 2 1

Dedication

To parents of children with special challenges:
May you find courage, joy, and REST!

and

To parents who have lost children:
May you grieve well,
remember well,
hope well

Contents

Acknowledgments

The fingerprints of many people are all over the pages of this book. I want to express thanks for those who helped:

—to Leonard Allen, my publisher and friend, who promised me that he'd help me make this book happen if I wanted to write it;

—to Greg Taylor, whose amazing editing and writing skills were essential from the early conceptualization (on napkins at a burger place) to the final words;

—to Karen Hill, Sherry Rankin, Darryl Tippens, Sara Barton, Max Lucado, Josh Ross, and Stephen Weathers, who read the manuscript and provided feedback that made this a much better book than it would have been without their skill and wisdom;

—to Thom Lemmons, Lee Ann and Tod Brown, and Pam and Randy Cope for letting me share their writings and stories.

My thanks to the Heartbeat Team for giving me the time to write: Landon Saunders, my friend and coworker; and Bruce and Debbie Bixby, Leon and Margaret Blue, Jimmy and Andee Cone, Don and Rudith Drennan, Michael Hawkins, Phil and Annette Herrington, Gary and Millie Skidmore, Doug and Nan Smith, Steve and Kathy Stevens, Neika Stephens, Talmadge and Sara Trammell, and Don and Ellen Williams. A special word of thanks goes to Bruce, who two decades ago was the builder for our house in Abilene—Diane and I will never forget how he considered Megan's needs at every stage of the construction!—and who has now provided me space for writing and working.

I'm thankful to my wife, Diane, for letting me share parts of her private journal—and much more, of course, for loving and caring for Megan every second of her precious ten years. I'm grateful for our sons, Matt and Chris, who carry the joy of their sister inside them. Thanks, also, to Matt and my granddaughter Reese for quickly responding to my request to pose for the shot on the book's cover, and to Jenna, my daughter-in-law, for taking the photo. I hope that someday Reese and Ellie will find in these pages sweet memories of an aunt they never knew.

❊ ❊ ❊

One final note of thanks. This one is unusual.

Not long after my daughter died, my friend Leon Blue gave me a pen—a beautiful Montblanc, a pen I'd never buy for myself—and told me it was to write about Megan.

So the pen and I went to work in my journals. We wrote of grief, regret, and joy. We questioned God about her suffering; we thanked God for her life. Eventually, we began writing magazine articles about her.

Then the pen and I began work on *Megan's Secrets*. (I still prefer writing on a tablet before pulling out my Mac. Maybe it's because my mind and my pen were linked.)

Rarely did I travel with the pen for fear of losing it. But I took it with me to Atlanta to work on final edits just before the book was due to the publisher.

On the flight from Atlanta to DFW, I dropped it down the side of my seat. I saw where it went and began digging around looking for it. When I couldn't find it in the seat, I pulled the seat cushion off. Nothing. Then I got in the aisle on all fours and looked all around to see if it had rolled. This of course drew the attention of a flight attendant, who offered to help. We looked until it became a distraction. I said, "I'll wait until everyone deplanes and look then."

So I waited until all the other passengers were gone and then resumed looking. The flight attendant, who had seen the pen's cap, returned and said, "I understand why you're so concerned. A Montblanc!" That's when I told the story: "It's not that. A friend gave it to me when my daughter died to write about her. I've been doing that for fifteen years." The next thing I knew, three flight attendants were on their knees, fighting back tears, looking for my pen. Then the cleaning crew came on board to prepare the jet for the next flight and heard the story. Now six people were all but dismantling the plane (and did disassemble my seat) looking for it.

But to no avail. The pen was gone. Is gone. Either God called it home or someone decided to borrow it. After twenty minutes of searching every nook and cranny, we finally had to admit that we wouldn't find it.

So, thank you, my pen, my friend—for accompanying me through dark days. Thanks for suggesting words of hope. And thanks for staying with me until the writing assignment was finished. I hope you're in someone else's hands now. Perhaps there was someone with fresh grief on our flight who needed you more.

Introduction

When they hear me say it—that my mentally disabled daughter, Megan, was the most profound teacher I've had in my life—some people think I'm being maudlin. Or at least that I'm exaggerating for dramatic effect.

But I couldn't be more serious. This child who could only speak one sentence in her whole life taught me more than any of the wonderful professional teachers I've had.

Calculus, physics, foreign languages—these were never going to be in Megan's future. But she had a profound understanding of things that really matter in life: she forgave easily; she loved others unconditionally; and she drew people into a world of acceptance.

Of course, that isn't to say her life was easy. There were challenges for all of us every day. But even the challenges came with joy and exhausted laughter.

For example, Megan had one bad eye and one really bad eye, so for four hours a day, she had to wear a patch over the bad eye to try to strengthen the other one. She hated—detested!—that patch. It was a minute-by-minute battle to keep it on her.

Mondays were my special day with her while my wife, Diane, was taking classes. Megan's insistence and my lack of patience intersected on Mondays. And the point of intersection was the patch. I'd put it on her, and she'd rip it off the moment I looked the other way. I'd put it back on, she'd take it off. I'd put it on, she'd yank it off, put it in her mouth, and swallow it. So we'd start again.

One Monday I had an idea: get her so busy having fun that she'd forget about it. So into the backyard we went. We kicked the soccer ball, played on the swing set, ran with our dog—anything just to keep active!

After four hours, we went back inside, and I said, "Megan, you can take the patch off!" I collapsed on the couch, exhausted but satisfied at what a clever dad I'd been. I didn't think about how she would need a drink of water but wouldn't be able to ask for it.

I heard a sound from the other room: splash, splash, splash. I walked into the bathroom to find Megan lapping up water from the toilet. Her ladle was Diane's toothbrush. I was too tired to worry about it; I guess I thought, "What you don't know can't hurt you" (plus the toilet had just been cleaned), so I slung the water off the toothbrush and put it back in the toothbrush holder.

That evening, I walked into the bathroom to see Diane brushing her teeth. The laughter I'd been fighting back now came out like a locomotive. She looked at me strangely and asked, "What's so funny?"

I choked out the words, "Megan used your toothbrush in the toilet."

That's when she started laughing hysterically. I said, "What's so funny?"

Diane replied, "She usually uses yours."

Some people think I exaggerate Megan stories, but those who knew Megan know I under-tell the stories.

Ah, life with The Meg (as my mother called her).

But despite the challenges, despite the disappointments, despite the exhaustion (for she didn't waste much of her time sleeping—two or three hours a night was about it), life with Megan was joy-filled and enlightening. In her presence, the insanities of this world tended to be exposed.

I fully understand why Henri Nouwen left his teaching post at Harvard Divinity School to join the Daybreak community in Toronto. His decision to move from the respected halls of the academy to the mundane tasks of working among and with mentally disabled adults puzzled many. But it makes complete sense to me: he was seeking community and truth, and that's where he found it.

In his book *Adam*, he tells of his friendship with one of the residents. Following are a couple of the profound passages. I've just inserted "Megan" for "Adam."

> *Megan couldn't produce anything, had no fame to be proud of, couldn't brag of any award or trophy. But by her very life, she was the most radical witness to the truth of our lives that I have ever encountered.*
>
> *"Everyone who touched [Jesus] was healed" (Mark 6:56). Each of us who has touched Megan has been made whole somewhere; it has been our common experience.[1]*

That's not just schmaltzy talk from a father. When Megan died, I lost my daughter and my guide.

For ten years, I was this child's pupil as she modeled for me the love of God in Jesus Christ.

MEGAN DIANE COPE

Megan was born in Wilmington, North Carolina, in the summer of 1984, just before the arrival of a hurricane packing 110-mile-per-hour winds. Later, we learned to appreciate this heavenly omen.

For Megan was a hurricane. Her gale-force winds blew so hard through our lives that they sometimes tested our structural soundness. But she was also a refreshing breeze who for ten years blew the smog and pollution out of our hearts.

We've often said there were two Megans: the robust, muscular little girl who lived in Arkansas (where we moved shortly after her birth), and the medically fragile child who eventually was on oxygen twenty-four hours a day in Texas (where we moved in 1991).

"Arkansas Megan" spent every waking hour—which was nearly every single hour—singing, marching, and cleaning out every drawer and closet in the house.

Though there were clear, early indications that Megan had developmental problems, Diane and I were blind to them. We knew she had mild scoliosis, vision problems, and a slight asymmetry in her face, though it was hard to tell because people got lost in her beautiful eyes and didn't notice; and we knew she wasn't catching on to speech very easily.

Actually, she talked all the time and seemed to know exactly what she was saying. We just didn't understand! Our son Matt decided when his sister was three or four that she was probably speaking Chinese and was actually precocious instead of slow.

When she discovered or created a phrase, she'd ride it. We went through the SHEGAH stage, which came with the related SHECOME and SHEGO. She realized she could get a laugh in public by saying, "Mad!" So "mad" joined her small repertoire of words. Another was a mild obscenity which she would say at the top of her lungs, especially at church. It was her closest attempt at saying "Diane!"

Imagine a preacher's kid marching around the church building at the age of five yelling, "Damn!"

But our denial about her condition came to a heartbreaking halt in 1989 when a pediatric specialist pronounced the diagnosis: "Megan isn't just delayed. Her brain functioning isn't normal. She's mentally disabled."

A geneticist informed us that Megan likely had a rare genetic syndrome called Goldenhar. With that word, with that prognosis, our tidy little planned world buckled.

I'll never forget the stunned look on Diane's face, and I could only imagine the look on mine. I couldn't really feel my face. The numbness of that news shocked me speechless. We stammered through a few questions to the doctor and could hardly speak on the way home. This was not the news we ever would have imagined. Would Megan ever go through the rites of passage that we'd envisioned: graduation, marriage, parenting?

Like so many other parents, we adjusted, trusting God to give us the strength and wisdom we'd need for the coming days. We had already learned from Jesus the importance of loving the "least among us"; but amazingly, our lives, though challenging, would be enriched as we set aside what didn't really matter and focused on Megan's needs.

About the time we moved to Texas, however, her health took a downhill slide. She was hit first by a severe case of chicken pox, then by encephalitis, and then by a serious reaction to one of the medicines that controlled her seizures.

For the last three years of her life, Megan was medically fragile as she faced bout after bout of aspiration pneumonia. We moved from one ER to another, sometimes in a car, at other times on a medical emergency plane.

We did our best to learn how to care for her—Diane became her primary "nurse"—learning how to clean her sinuses with salt water, how to loosen stuff in her lungs with a percussor, how to use the G-button that was put in her stomach, and how to take constant readings of her oxygen level. (I have kept in my desk three 8½ by 11 pages of instructions Diane wrote that explained the daily regimen of care.)

Even now I hate that we couldn't adequately explain to Megan why we did all that prodding and poking, why we wouldn't let her have a glass of liquid, why she had to drag around tubes. Yet through it all, she looked at us in absolute trust and continued to bless all who came near her with wordless power.

Just before she took her final breaths, we gathered around her as I spoke these words over her (with language that reflected her favorite song from Sunday school, "I'm in the Lord's Army"):

Megan,

You have been a blessing from God for ten years. You have worn us out—but much more, you have taught us about the deeper meanings of life. With your joy, your love, and your pure spirit, you have challenged our petty complaints about life.

Just as you have lived with great joy, may you die with the joy and peace of the Lord upon you. You have always wanted to march in the Lord's army. Your mother, your brothers, these friends, and I all release you into his hands. Please save a place in the ranks for us, for we will always look forward to seeing you again.

May the Lord bless you and keep you;

May the Lord make his face shine upon you and be gracious to you;

May the Lord turn his face toward you and give you peace.

OUR LITTLE YODA

As challenging as her decade of life was, our little Yoda instructed us without words, guided us without sentences, and mentored us in the way of God's peaceable kingdom. Megan became one of those "little ones" who can't articulate theology but who are for us living, breathing icons of Christ's admonition to take no thought for tomorrow but simply, in faith, to let each day unfold on its own.

Early on, as parents, we tend to focus on what we might pass on to our children, what we can teach them. As life with Megan unfolded, we learned far more from her than we could ever teach.

The first half of this book, focusing on the first two "secrets," is about the power of her life—a frail, fragile, broken life. The second half pushes further into themes of loss, joy, doubt, faith, grief, and hope. I've realized as I've written this book that these "secrets" became more obvious as we faced other tidal waves of loss.

So—what did we learn from Megan? What were her "secrets"? That's what I want to pass along in this book.

First Secret

GOD IS A HEART SPECIALIST

I am often asked to describe the experience of raising a child with a disability—to try to help people who have not shared that unique experience to understand it, to imagine how it would feel. It's like this. . . .

When you're going to have a baby, it's like planning a fabulous vacation trip—to Italy. You buy a bunch of guide books and make your wonderful plans. The Coliseum. The Michelangelo David. The gondolas in Venice. You may learn some handy phrases in Italian. It's all very exciting.

After months of eager anticipation, the day finally arrives. You pack your bags and off you go. Several hours later, the plane lands. The stewardess comes in and says, "Welcome to Holland."

"Holland?!?" you say. "What do you mean Holland?? I signed up for Italy! I'm supposed to be in Italy. All my life I've dreamed of going to Italy."

But there's been a change in the flight plan. They've landed in Holland and there you must stay.

The important thing is that they haven't taken you to a horrible, disgusting, filthy place, full of pestilence, famine and disease. It's just a different place.

So you must go out and buy new guide books. And you must learn a whole new language. And you will meet a whole new group of people you would never have met.

It's just a different place. It's slower-paced than Italy, less flashy than Italy. But after you've been there for a while and you catch your breath, you look around . . . and you begin to notice that Holland has windmills . . . and Holland has tulips. Holland even has Rembrandts.

But everyone you know is busy coming and going from Italy . . . and they're all bragging about what a wonderful time they had there. And for the rest of your life, you will say "Yes, that's where I was supposed to go. That's what I had planned."

And the pain of that will never, ever, ever, ever go away . . . because the loss of that dream is a very, very significant loss.

But if you spend your life mourning the fact that you didn't get to Italy, you may never be free to enjoy the very special, the very lovely things . . . about Holland.

—"Welcome to Holland," by Emily Perl Kingsley

1

Looking for a Few Good Eggs

I gave this mite a gift I denied to all of you—eternal innocence. . . . She will never offend me, as all of you have done. She will never pervert or destroy the works of my Father's hands. She is necessary to you. She will evoke the kindness that will keep you human. . . . This little one is my sign to you. Treasure her![1]

—MR. ATHA (the returned Christ) speaking of a child with Down Syndrome in Morris West's *The Clowns of God*

A while back, I read an essay in *Atlantic Monthly* by Jessica Cohen, a Yale University student. She told about spotting a classified ad in the *Yale Daily News*: EGG DONOR NEEDED.

The couple placing the ad was looking for an egg from just the right donor, and they were willing to pay big bucks, to the tune of twenty-five thousand dollars. She learned that they wanted an Ivy League university student who was over 5 feet 5 inches tall, of Jewish heritage, athletic, and attractive and who had a minimum combined SAT score of 1500.

Being a bit short on cash, Cohen thought she might follow the lead. Cohen began corresponding with the anonymous couple. And as she did, she was introduced to a whole world of online ads by such desperate couples. She found one website with five hundred classifieds posted. An eBay for genetic material, she thought. Plus, there were ads like the following from young women wanting to sell their eggs:

> Hi! My name is Kimberly. I am 24 years old, 5'11" with blonde hair and green eyes. I previously donated eggs and the couple was blessed with BIG twin boys! The doctor told me I have perky ovaries! . . . The doctor told me I had the most perfect eggs he had ever seen.

Cohen's e-mails with the husband were strange. He and his wife were concerned about her scores in science and math. Then she sent a few pictures they had requested. The husband responded: "I showed the pictures to [my wife] this a.m. Personally, I think you look great. She said ho-hum."

After that, Cohen's correspondence with the couple abruptly ended.[2]

What kind of bizarre world is this? Our culture is fascinated with the "accidents" of birth: looks, athletic ability, and IQ. What if volcanic ash suddenly covered the United States, and it wasn't until centuries later that archaeologists dug down to uncover our civilization, but the only written material they could locate were magazines from the checkout counters of grocery stores? What would those archaeologists assume about us? Maybe that we were the most shallow group of people ever?

This world of genetic engineering would favor my sons. But who—in our success-driven world—would want my daughter's genetic makeup? She was, after all, mentally disabled. She would never take the SAT test, she wasn't headed toward an Ivy League school, and chances were really good she wasn't going to be over 5'5"! She couldn't produce anything, had no fame to be proud of, and couldn't brag of any trophies. We have classes in schools for "gifted and talented" students. By that standard, my daughter wasn't very successful.

And yet she was the most radical witness to the love of God I've ever met. She changed our world. I wonder: What if our society awarded friendliness, forgiveness, endurance, joyfulness, and unconditional love?

Megan was a quiet, loving witness to the gospel. She was an incarnation of God's love. She received whatever gifts of service we offered to her without expecting more. She embodied the truth of 2 Corinthians 4:7: "But we have this treasure in jars of clay to show that this all-surpassing power is from God and not from us."

Let the world search for "the perfect egg." But our eyes have been opened by the breaking through of the kingdom in Jesus Christ. We've heard him say, "God bless you—you who are poor in spirit. God bless you—you who mourn. And God bless you—you who are meek."

One of Megan's much older friends was inspired by her life and wrote the following about her:

Megan proclaimed her message in her life. She was a walking icon of Christ's admonition to take no thought for tomorrow, but simply, in faith, to let each day unfold on its own. I doubt it ever occurred to Megan to make long-range plans or to fear what the next five minutes might bring. Megan, like the birds of the air and the lilies of the field, trusted in the Creator, through his human agents, to supply whatever requirements she might have. She knew no other way to live. And in that respect, she sits in judgment on us all, and leads us toward a more primitive and perfect trust.

So many people were drawn to Megan. I think many college students in particular were drawn to her because they were being constantly bombarded everywhere else with messages about who they were supposed to be in order to be successful in this life. And the powerful reminder they always received from being with Megan was that success has more to do with internal qualities of the heart than with external circumstances and accidents of birth.

A society reveals a lot about itself by what it esteems and rewards. Apparently, we tend to value accidents of birth that we chisel and hone into perfection, then put on display—and even then we airbrush out the imperfections: how you look in a swimsuit, what you score on your SAT, how fast you can run a forty-yard dash.

No wonder so many people end up feeling bad about themselves. Some express this in self-loathing, others in arrogance. We watch anorexic models on television who've had surgical assistance with their shape, and we start feeling bad about ourselves. We often feel we're too short, too tall, too wide, too skinny, hips too big, hips too small, curve too much, don't curve enough. No wonder plastic surgery is such a booming business. Convince enough people that they are a mess as they are now, and you have an endless supply of business.

Megan had a way of exposing the insanity of all this craziness. As my friend Thom Lemmons said:

> *Megan was a flesh-and-blood display of the topsy-turvy economy of the kingdom of heaven. She was one of the least of us, yet she occupied the apex of our care, absorbing all the loving service we could offer, and able to absorb still more. Without any thank you, without any false reticence, without even seeming to notice, she took all that we could give her, and still we were left with the sense that it was not enough.*
>
> *And yet, to anyone who held her down for a breathing treatment, or marched with her through the church parking lot, singing, "I'm in the Lord's army. Yes, sir!" or changed her soiled undergarments, or tried in vain to rescue some semi-edible artifact from her unbelievably quick hands, or held her as she gasped for breath—to anyone who ever poured a minute's worth of love down the bottomless pit that was Megan, the blessing that followed beggared any other reward.*
>
> *Megan taught us all the difference in value between receiving and giving. We only wished we could have done more: there was no question of doing less. And all the while, we were the ones being made over—by her innocent carelessness and her shattering need—into a closer imitation of the One who poured out his life as a ransom for many.*

One day, Thom and Cheryl Lemmons were taking care of Megan at a time when she needed oxygen to survive. Thom describes how he thought he'd figured out a secret to Megan's care.

The trick was to keep Megan within a short enough radius of her oxygen tank to permit the tubes to stay in her nostrils and simultaneously remain connected to the hose. She was also prone to seizures then, but I didn't know that. At one point, I remember having her in my lap on the floor of the living room, and I may have even been singing to her. For a few moments, the ceaseless thrashing stopped, the grasping fingers were still, and she stared up into my face with what appeared to me as a beatific half-smile. Then, after a minute or two, we resumed the Greco-Roman wrestling match. "What a wonderful, peaceful, very brief interlude," I thought, as I put her oxygen tubes back in place for the 5,357th time, "no doubt, made possible by my instinctive gentleness and boundless patience. Surely, even Megan is not immune to my gifts."

Later, over lunch, I was relating to the Copes and Cheryl my moment of epiphany with Megan, there on the living room floor. Diane got a slightly embarrassed look as I described the scene. Cheryl leaned over to me and whispered, "Thom, she wasn't listening to you sing; she was having a seizure."

Classic Megan: if ever your sense of "Christian duty" became self-congratulatory or the least bit inflated by a sense of its own worth, Megan would simply leave you holding the punctured bag, and allow you to deal with your own deflated ego. Megan, how could we ever repay all that you taught us?

Megan's simple-yet-profound life reminded us that God is a heart specialist who looks deeper than accidents of birth.

On the day she died, Diane and I were leaning over her praying for her, telling her we loved her, and assuring her it was all right to go. We almost forgot that anyone else was in the room. But the moment she took her last breath in the pediatric intensive care unit, my mother stood up from her chair behind us and began singing Megan's favorite song:

> *I may never march in the infantry,*
> *ride in the cavalry,*
> *shoot the artillery.*
> *I may never fly o'er the enemy,*
> *but I'm in the Lord's army.*

Later it hit me: Megan had been preparing us her whole life with her simple little song. It's like she'd been telling us that there were many things she'd never do, but we shouldn't worry, because she's in the Lord's army. There's a little grave just outside Abilene that bears her name, the dates of her abbreviated life, and then the words "I'm in the Lord's army."

This tiny minister taught me more than I learned in ninety hours of graduate school. She taught me that God will use my brokenness to his glory. She reminded me that the power is God's, not mine. She made me remember we are often fascinated with things that are impressive from the outside but which may not be that important to God. She taught me that what really matters has to do with the heart: keeping promises, seeking justice in a brutal world, learning to see those in greatest need, and living with courage, joy, and unconditional love.

Now, years later, my diminutive instructor-daughter is still guiding me.

2

A (Runt of a) Man after God's Own Heart

*David provides a large chunk of the evidence that
disabuses us of the idea that perfection is part of the job
description of the men and women who follow Jesus. More
narrative space is given in our Scriptures to the story of
David than to any other single person, and there are no
perfectionist elements in it. The way of David is, from
start to finish, a way of imperfection.*[1]

—Eugene Peterson

Each year, people in the United States spend eight billion dollars—
that's $8,000,000,000!—on beauty products. I point this out not to
shame us for using makeup or too much shampoo—although rinsing and repeating does seem a little over the top—but because these
purchases indicate what is highly valued in our culture. We spend
money on what we value, and clearly beauty is near the top.

This focus on outward appearance is not limited to the United
States, nor is it limited to the twenty-first century. Even in the
Ancient Near East, people were prone to choose leaders by how
tall and handsome they were (as with Saul, the first king of Israel),

and queens were chosen by how stunningly beautiful they looked (as seen in the story of Esther in Persia).

So when the prophet Samuel came to Jesse's house to find a successor to King Saul, even the priest-prophet Samuel was inclined to choose based on the physical qualities of the sons. Samuel saw Eliab and, impressed with his features, assumed that this surely must be the anointed one. First-round draft pick.

To say that David was a dark horse candidate would be to overestimate his chances. His own father didn't even mention him in the beginning when Samuel was examining his sons.

Had Samuel seen Michelangelo's *David*—his image burned into the collective consciousness of the Western world, tall and handsome, covered with chiseled muscles that would have made him a prime candidate for *People* magazine's "50 Sexiest Men"—he would have been a shoo-in for Israel's second king. The David statue is stunning and stops people short when they first see it. He's a ripped piece of marble, the ideal man. This David of Florence would have made the perfect King Número Dos of Israel. Those are just the criteria the prophet Samuel was using as he searched in the household of Jesse for the new leader.

The story of finding Israel's second-ever king reminds us again of this first secret that a country spending eight billion dollars annually on cosmetics needs to hear: In a world where people look at the external qualities of a person, God is a heart specialist who values those qualities that have little to do with what people look like, how they perform, and how smart they are.

There are six hundred occurrences of David's name in the Old Testament and sixty others in the New Testament. But aside from the genealogy at the end of Ruth, 1 Samuel 16 is the first time he's mentioned. And he's not even referred to by name until well into the story. His father, Jesse, simply refers to him as "the youngest who is off tending sheep."

David doesn't get the nod because he's the smartest, oldest, or most powerful. The story is more an affirmation of the wisdom of Galadriel, Tolkien's Elf Queen, to the "halfling" Frodo: "Even the smallest person can change the course of the future."

We can still understand the dynamic of this story well. For we live in a culture that broadcasts nonstop messages about how we ought to look. These 24-7 ads make this very clear: we need something we don't have in order to be successful. Our bodies need to be thinner, curvier, stronger, tanner. We're told we are one product away from a happier, healthier life with lots of friends, wealth, and success. As Barbara Dafoe Whitehead has noted, the fashion magazines that young girls often consult well into their twenties send one clear message: "Your body is a mess." No wonder studies show that by age thirteen, fifty-three percent of the girls in the United States are unhappy with their bodies, and by the time they're seventeen, seventy-eight percent are displeased.[2]

These messages tell us that thick hair, thin waists, and six-pack abs will drive others crazy with desire. Recently in my local newspaper, there was a half-page ad that screamed, "Grow back sexy thick hair." It asks (but seems to already know the answer): "Do you secretly worry that your thinning hair will gradually get worse and worse . . . and that eventually you'll become bald and 'invisible' to women?" The product claims that it's perfect for you if you want a quick and easy solution to "your hair loss problem so you'll look and feel sexy, younger, and more confident."

I'm a guy with a hole in my head—a bald spot on my pate that's shaped like a yarmulke. I should be their ideal candidate, but instead I'm their worst nightmare. I don't care! It's just hair. As Tony Campolo has always said, "Men are only given so many hormones. If some guys want to use theirs for growing hair, that's their business!"

This cultural idea—"sexy thick hair"—has nothing to do with a biblical ideal of what it means to be a true human being.

That's what God said to Samuel when he was choosing a new king to anoint.

"But the Lord said to Samuel, 'Do not consider his appearance or his height, for I have rejected him. The Lord does not look at the things human beings look at. People look at the outward appearance, but the Lord looks at the heart.'"[3]

Anne Lamott, one of the most downright honest writers today, tells this humorous, self-effacing episode about going to the beach with her "aunties" (her nickname for her thighs) and "letting it all hang out."

After adequate self-talking, she decided that she and the aunties—who'd "been held captive in a dark closet too long"—would go for a walk. She enjoyed seeing children, including her son, splashing around in the ocean and playing with the sand.

It was on her way back to her room for a nap that all the good feelings disintegrated, as she explains:

And then out of nowhere, like dogs from hell, four teenage girls walked toward me to wait for a van.

They weren't wearing cover-ups either, but they were lovely and firm as models—I'd say that was the main difference—and all in bikinis. Two of them were already perfectly tan. And suddenly my trance was broken. Suddenly it was the Emperor's New Clothes, and I stood there in all of my fatitude like the tubby little emperor with his feta-cheese gut. . . . I wanted a trapdoor to open at my feet. And then—this is the truth—they looked at me. . . . But then they made a fatal mistake. They looked at each other with these amused looks—the kind I must have given flabby women in swimsuits thirty years ago. And it gave me time to have two thoughts. One was not even a thought exactly: I just looked directly back at the four of them and heard the phantom clock playing in the background of their lives, "Tick, tock . . . tick, tock."

The other was the realization that I knew their secret: that they didn't think they were OK. They were already in the hyper self-consciousness of the American teenage girl, and this meant that they were doomed. The smallest one probably thought she was too short, the other one too tall. The most beautiful one had no breasts, the buxom one had crisp thin hair.

My heart softened, and I could breathe again (although I would have killed for a sarong). I felt deep compassion for them; I wanted to tell them the good news—that at some point you give up on ever looking much better than you do. Somehow, you get a little older, a little fatter, and you end up going a little easier on yourself. Or a lot easier. And I no longer felt ugly, maybe just a little ridiculous. I held my head a bit higher; I touched the aunties gently, to let them know I was there, and that made me less afraid. Ugliness is creeping around in fear, I remembered. Yet here I was, almost naked, *and—to use the medical term—flabbier than s***, but deeply loyal to myself.*[4]

Not surprisingly, many of the people who come the closest to "perfect" feel the worst about their bodies. The more you are obsessed with your body, the more you realize it falls short of perfection. There is probably more body-anxiety at the local gym than at the local bait shop.

No one is immune to the forces of rival stories that counter God's story of shaping us from within. We get these messages early in childhood from stories meant to entertain and teach. The edges have been sanded off of some of the original tales, but one message seems to come through again and again. Beauty may be down for the count, dead in a box, scrubbing the floor, or paired with a beast, but she always wins.

We tell our children they can do anything, even be president if they want someday. Our stories serve important functions of teaching virtue, but often stories inadvertently teach that virtue is not as important as kissing the object of your affection at the end. After all, what's the difference between Cinderella and the wicked stepsisters? She was the beauty! And speaking of beauty, Sleeping Beauty is awakened after one hundred years by the kiss of the prince. Lucky for her she wasn't Sleeping Ugly.

And what about Snow White? The dwarfs think she's dead, so they put her body in a glass coffin. Snow White is so beautiful, even dead. Then the prince comes along and asks for the body so he can stay close to her. (Can we agree that the prince has some issues that need to be explored?) Even the ugly duckling—in the redeeming moment—becomes a beautiful swan.

Instead of seeing ourselves as fearfully and wonderfully made, instead of focusing on character, we obsess on externals. This leads to lots of self-rejection and, on the other hand, arrogance. And arrogance is not always what it seems to be on the outside. Often, what we take as arrogance in other people is their attempt to avoid being seen as they see themselves.

While we obsess over accidents of birth—like what people look like on a runway in a swimsuit—God is looking at the heart. That's what Scripture keeps pointing us to—what kind of person we are becoming. To the religious leaders who loved appearances, money, and conspicuous wealth, Jesus said, "You are the ones who justify yourselves in the eyes of others, but God knows your hearts. What people value highly is detestable in God's sight."[5]

What kind of person, then, was David? Barbara Brown Taylor asks: "Was David a good man or a bad man? You decide. I think he was both, as most of us are."[6]

People often shine the exterior, obsess and brag about what we can see. If people were apples, we might be obsessed with the shiny red, green, or yellow skins of the apple, but a healthy, shiny, crunchy, juicy apple does not get to be that way on its own. Jesus also said:

> *Make a tree good and its fruit will be good, or make a tree bad and its fruit will be bad, for a tree is recognized by its fruit. You brood of vipers, how can you who are evil say anything good? For out of the overflow of the heart the mouth speaks. Good people bring good things out of the good stored up in them, and evil people bring evil things out of the evil stored up in them. But I tell you that people*

will have to give account on the day of judgment for every
empty word they have spoken. For by your words you will
be acquitted, and by your words you will be condemned.
(Matt. 12:33–37)

We spend lots of time polishing our fruit, shining up a few apples off of withering trees, when the exhortation of our Lord is to support and nurture the tree, the root system, the water and fertilizer that produce good fruit. Later, Jesus gives another example with the same focus on the heart.

"Are you still so dull?" Jesus asked them. "Don't you see that whatever enters the mouth goes into the stomach and then out of the body? But the things that come out of the mouth come from the heart, and these defile you. For out of the heart come evil thoughts, murder, adultery, sexual immorality, theft, false testimony, slander. These are what defile you; but eating with unwashed hands does not defile you."[7]

When David was chosen as king of Israel, he was a runt, an also-ran who didn't even make the lineup of choices. But even before he took the throne, God had made it clear that it was the size of a leader's heart that mattered—not the size of his biceps.[8]

Not only was David's physique not the perfect Michelangelo image (though even the writer of this account notes that he was "glowing with health and had a fine appearance and handsome features"), but his life and his choices were flawed and imperfect as well. David was not distinguished for his looks, or his perfect political or personal record; rather, God affirmed him for his heart. Centuries later, the apostle Paul elaborated on the choice to his synagogue audience in Antioch: "After removing Saul, God made

David their king. God testified concerning him: 'I have found David son of Jesse, a man after my own heart; he will do everything I want him to do.'"[9]

This is the secret we learned from Megan—that God is a heart specialist.

With her simplicity, she taught us not to be consumed by 401(k)s or IRAs. We still laugh at Christmas when we open presents, remembering that Megan much preferred the wrapping paper and the boxes to whatever may have been inside the boxes. We learned eventually to put an extra roll of wrapping paper under the tree, just so she could tear off little pieces and crinkle them. It's so easy in our culture to make Christmas about the gifts and the perfect meals—we forget what's really important: love and time spent in joy with one another. Megan taught us that.

With her understated joy, we learned to quit being so embarrassed about everything. I remember one time we were at a pizza restaurant. We had learned to sit Megan in a chair facing away from others in restaurants because she tended to grab anyone else's food if she saw and liked it. I can still see it playing out in slow motion: she scraped the topping off a piece of pizza and then flung the rest over her shoulder. It landed, tomato paste side down, on the light blouse of a university student at the next table. I was so embarrassed that I jumped up and offered to buy the student a new blouse, but she just laughed and said, "That's how I wish I could eat. I prefer the topping, too!"

I was amazed at the grace shown us by this young woman we'd never met. She saw Megan through God's eyes. I was embarrassed, but as it turned out, I had no need to be. Megan constantly created situations that forced us to accept the graciousness and tolerance of strangers; she brought out the best in other people, as well as in us.

With her love for just being together, we learned to sit next to her while she watched her video favorites: Sherry Lewis, Sesame Street, and Disney Sing-a-Long. (I'll surely never forget that it's a small world after all. I must have heard that song a million times.)

A favorite memory for me is walking in and seeing her with Chris by her side watching those videos. They were age appropriate for both, though one was ten and the other two! Megan, being so tactile, had a strange habit of holding an extra video and hitting the side of her head with it over and over. I don't know what to say except this: she liked the sensation. (As my father used to say, if you haven't tried it, don't knock it.) One day I walked in and Chris— who was learning from his beloved older sister—was doing the same thing. They were both hitting their skulls with a video. I said, "Chris, no! Don't hit your head with a video." He looked puzzled and said, "Megan?" It was hard to explain why it was all right for her but not for him.

She altered the world around her not because she was beautiful (though I'll never in my life see more beautiful eyes!), nor because of her brilliance. At least not the kind of brilliance that is measured by standardized testing.

We never could have put a bumper sticker on our car announcing that our daughter is an honors student. I can imagine some others that would have been fun: "Our daughter didn't pull anyone's hair at school last week!" or "Our daughter only tried to break out of her classroom twice today!"

The truth is that bumper sticker wisdom couldn't begin to contain Megan's insight. She spent her short decade of life by joyfully experiencing whatever the day might bring (yes, even during days of poor health) and by loving whoever might be around her.

3

All-Stars

Let me win. But if I cannot win,
let me be brave in the attempt.

—Motto of the Special Olympics

We had our tickets to Switzerland. I could already taste the cheese and chocolate, breathe the morning mountain air, and see the Alps in my mind's eye. Diane and I were going there with our dear friends Darryl and Anne Tippens for a spiritual retreat focusing on the theme of creation theology—a retreat that Darryl and I would be leading. The mountain hikes, the fresh air, the old and new friends—all would prove to be healing for us so soon (only seven months) after Megan's death.

The timing for travel is never exactly right, however, and this time we left right before the Little League all-stars were announced. That's a big deal around Abilene, Texas—bigger than it should be. My mom was staying with the boys, ages thirteen and two at the time. So I left her a note to give to Matt, who was an all-star hopeful. Though I thought Matt would be selected, I didn't know for sure. As a person who has coached Little League baseball for twelve years, I have learned this: We all think our children deserve to be all-stars!

My instructions to my mother were to deliver the letter after he received the news that he'd made all-stars. Here is what the letter said:

Dear Matt,

I'm writing this before I leave to congratulate you for making all-stars. You had such a great year. Your hitting, your fielding, your pitching—well, no wonder you're on the all-star team. We'll look forward to the games.

In my better moments, I've learned that God has used some of my disappointments to remind me of what is ultimately important. None of the standards of this life (batting averages, SAT scores, looks, etc.) ultimately matter. "The Lord does not look at the things human beings look at. People look at the outward appearance, but the Lord looks at the heart" (1 Samuel 16:7). It's important for you to remember this. You're one of the fortunate ones who's been blessed with looks, athletic ability, and intelligence.

But—ultimately—the standards our world sets for success are meaningless. Our silly culture has found a way to glorify shallow, selfish people while "pitying" people like your sister— those who don't "measure up." Something's terribly wrong with our understanding of what matters, don't you think?

My guess is that those rare people who experience no disappointments never have their eyes opened to see what matters in life.

So trust in the Lord, Matt, and love those who are around you. That's the only accurate measure of success.

But along the way, it's okay to enjoy honors like this! I'm very proud of you.

Love,
Dad

That's the letter my mom gave to him. What he didn't know until many years later is that I'd left two letters behind. They were almost identical. But the other one began, "I'm so sorry you didn't make all-stars."

I always tried to remember, as I coached the boys, that performance on the field isn't what life is about—not life as we've learned it from Jesus. I'm not saying I was always successful at remembering that, of course.

One time, Christopher was batting late in the game with game-winning runs on the bases. He was one of my most reliable hitters. But he struck out on a high fastball. (It's pathological that I can still remember the pitch, isn't it?) When he came back to the dugout, I summoned all my coaching wisdom and sniped, "Don't swing at the high ones!" He was just ten, and my words stung. He grabbed his glove to head out to the mound with tears rolling down his cheeks.

I thought to myself, "You idiot!" I wanted to grab him, hug him, and say, "It doesn't matter to me if you strike out every time . . . as long as there are not runners in scoring position."

I should have learned the lesson a decade before that from a kid we met in a park in Arkansas.

It had been one of those days when I was resenting Megan's condition. I had taken Matt and her to a baseball card show. There was nothing Matt would rather do at the time than look at, trade, or buy baseball cards, and there was nothing I wanted to do more than be with him.

But I couldn't be. I tried strolling Megan through the narrow aisles, but she kept grabbing legs and then started trying to reach the cardboard gems.

So out we went to the playground. That's where we met Jason, a six-year-old child for whom "Twenty Questions" was a way of life.

"Hey, what's your name?" the boy asked Megan.

"Her name is Megan," I told the boy.

"Hey, you can swing next to me!"

"Well, she can't handle that kind of swing very well," I said. "Let's try this one with a safety bar."

"Hey, you want to go in the tunnel with me?"

"Let me get her out of the swing and we'll see."

"Hey, how come you keep answering for her?"

I smiled at the boy's raw honesty. "Megan doesn't talk much," I said.

"She looks old enough to talk. Why doesn't she?"

"Have you ever heard of being retarded?"

"No. Why doesn't she talk?"

"Well, Megan is almost seven but in the way she thinks—and talks!—she is more like someone who's two."

"Hey, that's all right. Megan, let's go through the tunnel."

And they did.

I love it when theologians come in such compact size! Jason pretty much had it figured out. Our popular version of the all-American kid is inadequate: the whiz kid who reads at age three, the precocious student who gets into accelerated classes, the Little Leaguer who makes all-stars.

Not every child is an early reader, a spelling bee winner, or an Albert Pujols on the Little League field.

But "Hey, that's all right"—Jesus loves all the little children of the world, regardless of how they can perform on stage, what their batting average is, and whether or not they make all-stars. God looks at the heart. The Lord is a heart specialist who wants us in that ragtag band of fumbling followers.

4

The Conversion of the Older Brother

*Here I am this morning—sad, broken-hearted, still
bearing in my spirit the wounds of darkness. I confess
to you honestly that I have no wings with which to fly or
even any legs on which to run—but listen, by the grace of
God, I am still on my feet! I have not fainted yet. I have
not exploded in the anger of presumption, nor have I
keeled over into the paralysis of despair. All I am doing is
walking and not fainting, hanging in there, enduring with
patience what I cannot change but have to bear.[1]*

—John Claypool

Is there a better-known story in the world than the one recorded
in Luke 15—the story of the prodigal son?

A few years ago, my older son and I went to Guatemala for a
three-week intensive language school. The teaching was one-on-
one, and at the end, my young teacher asked me to tell her a story.
So I told her this old parable of Jesus.

Through the last half of the story, Catalina cried. (Friends have
suggested that my Spanish was so bad she felt like a failure!) I asked

about her emotions, and she told me that this was much like what was happening in her own family. Only in her family, her sister wanted to come home from Mexico, but her father wouldn't permit it. She had disappointed him in the past, and he refused to forgive her.

Amazingly, she'd never heard the parable before, and it did what the stories of Jesus must surely have done when his contemporaries heard them for the first time: caught her off guard by their insight, their power, and their hopeful imagination.

An important subplot in this story is often overlooked. Jesus seems to have told it not primarily for the sake of people like the young son who know they've failed and need God's grace but for those who think they do not need God's grace and who, therefore, worry about associating with people who've blown it.

Those like the older son in the story. Not only do we often overlook the older brother, but that's how he felt: overlooked.

When the older brother came in from the field and found that his brother had returned home, he was angry. Once again, family life seemed to revolve around the younger brother, even after he'd blown a good bit of the family wealth and had crawled home. What would it feel like for the older brother, the all-star son, to watch all this?

My guess is that we prefer to focus on the father or the younger son in the story because we can identify too much with the older son. Too often, we've nursed a grudge so long, we might miss that grudge if we cut it away from our hearts. And the cancer of resentment can choke out gratitude and make us believe we are the all-stars of our own lives. We think we deserve the trophy, the golden glove for catching the most sales at work, the home run title for knocking it out of the park in a church ministry.

I've tried to imagine how his story may have unfolded . . . what he might have learned as the decades passed by and as he discovered that his all-star status wasn't as golden as he had once thought. Maybe his story would have gone something like this. . . .

THE ELDER BROTHER'S CONVERSION

My three-score-and-ten years are tucked well behind me now. But I still remember the day like it was last week.

I was the perfect son, the model citizen, the child everyone figured would be an elder in the synagogue, revered by the whole Jewish community. I worked in the fields from morning until the sun set; I committed large sections of the Torah to memory; and, perhaps most importantly, I honored my elders—including, of course, my father.

Life with my younger brother was never easy. It was as if he came from different parents. He was born with a burden of discontentment. A kind of restlessness stirred inside him from his earliest days.

But even with all his uneasiness . . . even with all his conflicts with our parents . . . I was still dumbfounded when I heard that he'd asked my father for his inheritance. That was like saying, "Father, I resent the fact that you refuse to die. So I'm going to ask you to drop dead by going ahead and giving me my share of the property." At the time, I was incensed that he wasn't beaten and thrown out for that kind of disrespect. Who, in our proper Torah-keeping Jewish society, asks their father for his property? Would even the pagans do such a thing?

But rather than beat him or throw him out, my father signed over the land. And rather than work the land once it was his, my brother sold it. He sold the land. Our land. That piece of rock and dirt that had belonged to my father's father and to his father—back many generations. Did he understand that it was land that God had promised to our people so long ago? We were wandering Arameans, and he promised us land. Then we were slaves in Egypt, and he promised us land. This land. The whole area from Dan to Beersheba—but land that came down to little chunks of property like the one our family has owned for so long.

But in a moment, the deed was done; my brother was gone.

It was hard enough getting little bits of information back from travelers—information about how my brother went from the Big Spender with whom everyone wanted to schmooze to being a servant who fed pigs. Imagine: a proper Jewish boy, raised in the faith of Israel, now reduced to feeding unclean animals.

But much worse than hearing that was watching my father age so quickly. Lines on his forehead from expressions of hope each day as he looked down the road; lines of sadness on his cheeks from expressions of grief each evening when he realized that once again his other son hadn't returned. At the time, I burned with bitterness that my father couldn't just cut him loose and enjoy those of us who had decided to remain at home.

Then the day came. I was toiling away faithfully in the fields. I heard a faint whisper of music in the distance. I started walking toward the house only to discover that it was joyful, celebratory music. A party had broken out. I remember thinking, "I don't recall anyone announcing that there would be a festival today."

I summoned one of our servants and asked what was happening. He smiled and replied, "Your brother is back!" Then he explained that the special calf had been slain to mark the occasion—along with a special robe, a special ring, and special sandals to adorn the Feeder of Swine.

I nearly collapsed. No one had ever killed a special calf—or even a skinny goat—for me. No special robe. No special ring. And I'd been slaving away day after day, never disobeying my father even once.

I resented anything being given for this ne'er-do-well brother of mine. He'd spent his share. Everything else was *my* part of the inheritance. In one sense, it was my fattened calf that was killed.

On top of all the resentment, there was shame. For someone told me that people had seen my father run to greet him. My father: a respected elder in our community. Elders don't run. It's not right. It's shameful. Running is for children; it's a sign of youth. But for a grown man to run—it brought shame to our family.

So I belched out my vitriolic anger at my father: "This son of yours"—I couldn't bring myself to call him my brother—"who has squandered your property with prostitutes comes home, and you slay the fattened calf for him?"

He put his hand on my shoulder and answered me: "My son, you are always with me, and everything I have is yours. But we had to celebrate and be glad, because this brother of yours was dead and is alive again; he was lost and is found." He talked about Ezekiel's old vision of our people coming home from exile—bruised and worn—a vision where the valley of bones springs to life. "Your brother is back from the dead!" he exclaimed.

Even now I remember that in the following days, my poisonous bitterness seeped out. I usually claimed that my reasons were religious: How could we, as the chosen people of God, receive back into community with such fanfare someone who has failed God and failed us so completely? "What message will we be sending to the children of our village?" I asked. Wouldn't it be an extra incentive to them to act improperly? "If you want a party in your honor, then dishonor your family and your God!"

I'd like to tell you that we had this big blowup and that life then began to mend—a reunited family on a smaller plot of land. But it's never really that easy.

When the party ended and the adrenaline of joy ran out, there was the hard work of re-forming our world. There was the lack of trust . . . there were hurt feelings . . . there was my slow, Scripture-induced rage . . . but rising above all the hurt and pain was my father's keen gratitude for having both—both!—his sons around him.

I would have left had social obligations and financial security not demanded that I stay. But it was no longer a home to me; it was a compound. A prison. I began finding reasons to miss family meals. In fact, I became the missing brother: present in body but absent in spirit. My righteous hatred kept me at arm's length.

I'm now in my seventy-sixth year, and the next couple of decades blur together a bit. I continued doing all the right things: I married the right Jewish girl, we formed a proper Jewish marriage, I became a respected leader of the synagogue, and we raised six proper Jewish children.

My world remained holy. Secure. Certain. Obey and you'll be blessed; disobey and you'll be cursed.

And then . . . one day, my neat, proper world ended. The sun didn't rise. The stars fell. The water became bitter. One of my own children—my second son, my fourth child—came to me and asked for *his* inheritance. He was leaving, he said. He couldn't take our tight little world any longer. He couldn't bear the rules. He thought the synagogue was full of self-righteous hypocrisy. And he wasn't even sure if he believed in the God of the Exodus—but if God does exist, he said, he hopes this God is nothing like the people who claim to know God so well.

I'm tempted to say that I always imagined how strong and firm I'd be at a moment like this. But the truth is that I never imagined such a moment. I'd done everything right. By the book. By *the* book. But my secure reading of the scrolls ended that very moment.

Instead of anger flaring, my heart broke. There was no one to talk to—no one to share my grief with. Too many secure, Torah-protected worlds around me.

But then I recalled an old story. So I went to my aged father—he was then just about the age I am now. I poured out my pain, and he held me as I crumpled into his arms. I wept—the tears of a hurting father and the tears of one more prodigal who'd finally come home to *his* father. There were no "now you understands"—no "I told you sos"—just shared grief and tender love.

The years have now passed. Grandchildren have come into my house. Now even two children of my grandchildren. But it's not altogether a happy-ending story. Not yet, anyway.

For my son has not yet come home. But every afternoon, I sit by a tree that looks down the road. And I watch. Just in case. And though I'm aged, and though it's still entirely inappropriate in our little world, I'm ready to run.

Life goes on. You wouldn't say that I'm ignoring my family that surrounds me out of grief. We laugh; we find times to celebrate. We have music and we enjoy good meals.

But, just in case, I always make sure there is a specially fed calf in the pen.

JESUS LOVES ME!

I like imagining that the older brother discovered that God is a heart specialist and that accidents of birth do not bring the blessing. Attempting perfection—physical or spiritual—is not only impossible without God but also rots the soul by the misapprehension that we can attain something only God provides.

God looks at the heart, past the crusty, calloused pride of the all-star brother, past our attempts to lock in the blessings by beauty, status, and accidents of birth.

The older brother had all the right "accidents of birth," and yet he turns out to be more lost than the brother who left. Why? Because he could not forgive; he could not accept his father's unconditional love and find joy in the return of the brother he had lost.

Megan, with all the wrong "accidents of birth," was spiritually miles ahead of the elder brother. She knew how to love—how to give it without strings attached—and how to accept it without pride or embarrassment. She communicated that incredible unconditional love of God through her life and through a song she loved to sing, "Jesus Loves Me." With her limited vocabulary, the only part of the song she actually sang was "LOVES ME!" She would march, clap, and make noises during the rest of the song. But she joined in heartily at her phrase:

Others: Yes, Jesus
Megan: LOVES ME!
Others: Yes, Jesus
Megan: LOVES ME!
Others: Yes, Jesus
Megan: LOVES ME!
Others (with Megan waiting to start again): The Bible tells
me so

Second Secret

Weak Is the New Strong

I have a bright, talented, and very funny friend in Seattle named Carolyn Martin. But Carolyn has cerebral palsy, and it is the particular tragedy of her condition that its outward signs—drooling, floppy arm movements, inarticulate speech, a bobbing head—cause people who meet her to wonder if she is retarded. Actually, her mind is the one part of her that works perfectly; it is muscular control that she lacks.

Carolyn lived for fifteen years in a home for the mentally retarded, because the state had no other place for her. Her closest friends were people like Larry, who tore off all his clothes and ate the institution's houseplants, and Arlene, who only knew three sentences and called everyone "Mama." Carolyn determined to escape from that home and to find a meaningful place for herself in the outside world.

Eventually, she did manage to move out and establish a home of her own. There, the simplest chores posed an overwhelming challenge. It took her three months to learn to brew a pot of tea and pour it into cups without scalding herself. But Carolyn mastered that feat and many others. She enrolled in high school, graduated, then signed up for community college.

Everyone on campus knew Carolyn as "the disabled person." They would see her sitting in a wheelchair, hunched over, painstakingly typing out notes on a device called a Canon Communicator. Few felt comfortable talking with her; they could not follow her jumbled sounds. But Carolyn persevered, stretching out a two-year Associate of Arts degree program over seven years. Next, she enrolled in a Lutheran college to study the Bible. After two years there, she was asked to speak to her fellow students in chapel.

Carolyn worked many hours on her address. She typed out the final draft—at her average speed of forty-five minutes a page—and asked her friend Josee to read it for her. Josee had a strong, clear voice.

On the day of the chapel service Carolyn sat slumped in her wheelchair on the left side of the platform. At times her arms jerked uncontrollably, her head lolled to one side so that it almost touched her shoulder, and a stream of saliva sometimes ran down her blouse. Beside her stood Josee, who read the mature and graceful prose Carolyn had composed, centered around this Bible text: "But we have this treasure in jars of clay to show that this all-surpassing power is from God but not from us."[1]

—Philip Yancey

5

"I'm Megan": When Your Resume Is Rejected

*Laura is going to be important for all of us in the family.
We have never had a "weak" person among us. We all
are hardworking, ambitious, and successful people who
seldom have had to experience powerlessness. Now Laura
enters and tells us a totally new story, a story of weakness,
brokenness, vulnerability, and total dependency. Laura,
who always will be a child, will teach us the way of Christ
as no one will ever be able to do.[1]*

—HENRI NOUWEN, to his family when he learned that his
sister-in-law had given birth to a baby girl with Down
Syndrome

During his missionary journeys, Paul was convinced that a
beachhead of the kingdom was needed in cities like Corinth,
a center of philosophy that had a port where ships docked on their
trade routes. Lots of sailors, soldiers, and traders passed through
the port of Corinth, and perhaps this was Paul's early attempt at
going viral, not on YouTube but through a portal where people
came and went to other portals.

From Paul's letters to the church in Corinth that we have, we can tell that his relationship with them was deep but conflictual.

Apparently, some people in the church in Corinth didn't think the traveling apostle was sufficiently impressive. He's not much of a televangelist, not all that polished, not telegenic, not skilled in delivery, not trained in rhetoric, some were saying. Given the long tradition of rhetorical training in the city of Corinth, how could their go-to guide be someone so commonplace?

In essence, they were rejecting Paul's bio.

That happened to me one time. I got my biographical sketch "rejected."

I've spoken a lot at Pepperdine University through the years for convocations. One time, there was a new dean who was really trying to "sell" the speakers to the students. He asked us all to send in short biographies that would tell them about us. However, mine came boomeranging back with this note:

> *Mike,*
>
> *Here are a few examples from last semester. Each one includes a short quote from the speaker. Thanks for taking time to re-do your bio.*
>
> *Steve Arrington's story begins in the jungles of Vietnam where he is introduced to marijuana. That faulty step shatters his Navy career as a bomb disposal frogman, plunges him into the underworld of drug smuggling, and sentences him to the terrors of prison. There amid brutal inmates and stifling depression, Steve discovers hope through a life-changing relationship with God. He is soon in deep water again. But this time surrounded by great white sharks as chief diver for the Cousteau Society. "I*

went from a world of darkness into an incredible new life!" Steve says. He was given a second chance and now dedicates his life to reaching people with a message of hope—daring them to go for their dreams.

Bernice King was only five years old when her father, civil rights leader Dr. Martin Luther King, Jr., was assassinated. Today she has amazed herself by following in her father's footsteps by becoming a minister. Author of Hard Questions, Heart Answers, *King continues her father's legacy by speaking against the persisting challenge of racism and challenging people to make her father's dream a reality. Says King, "Look, we have a problem. We really need to sit down and dig into it and deal with it . . . ultimately, racism is a spiritual issue." In Bernice's voice you'll hear echoes of the late Dr. King, but the vision is now her own.*

Sue Thomas at the age of eighteen months was watching television with her family when she suddenly went deaf. Sue responded by turning up the volume full blast and was sent to her room. The next day, realizing there was something drastically wrong, Sue's parents took her to the hospital where they learned that nothing could restore her hearing loss. Since then, Sue has spent endless hours working with voice and drama coaches. Because of her outstanding lip-reading ability, Sue eventually worked for the FBI as an undercover surveillant. "My mother explained that with God's help, there was absolutely nothing in my life I couldn't do."

I had to admit: those were good! I'd love to send one just like that. The problem, however, was that I had never been the chief diver for the Cousteau Society, I'd never been an undercover surveillant for the FBI, and I didn't come from an internationally famous family. I grew up in Mayberry!

So I sent a new one back. Mine said, tongue in cheek: "Mike Cope's spiritual crisis begins in a Vacation Bible School classroom when he realizes he hates the song, 'Booster, Booster, Be a Booster.'" The dean, who was just trying to do his job and was good-natured about it all, simply laughed.

Paul's CV had been rejected by the Christians in Corinth. So, in response, he writes five little biographical sketches:

Already you have all you want! Already you have become rich! You have begun to reign—and that without us! How I wish that you really had begun to reign so that we also might reign with you! For it seems to me that God has put us apostles on display at the end of the procession, like those condemned to die in the arena. We have been made a spectacle to the whole universe, to angels as well as to human beings. We are fools for Christ, but you are so wise in Christ! We are weak, but you are strong! You are honored, we are dishonored! To this very hour we go hungry and thirsty, we are in rags, we are brutally treated, we are homeless. We work hard with our own hands. When we are cursed, we bless; when we are persecuted, we endure it; when we are slandered, we answer kindly. We have become the scum of the earth, the garbage of the world—right up to this moment. (1 Cor. 4:8–13)

But we have this treasure in jars of clay to show that this all-surpassing power is from God and not from us. We are hard pressed on every side, but not crushed; perplexed, but not in despair; persecuted, but not abandoned; struck down, but not destroyed. We always carry around in our

*body the death of Jesus, so that the life of Jesus may also
be revealed in our body. For we who are alive are always
being given over to death for Jesus' sake, so that his life
may also be revealed in our mortal body. So then, death is
at work in us, but life is at work in you. (2 Cor. 4:7–12)*

*We put no stumbling block in anyone's path, so that
our ministry will not be discredited. Rather, as servants
of God we commend ourselves in every way: in great
endurance; in troubles, hardships and distresses; in
beatings, imprisonments and riots; in hard work, sleepless
nights and hunger; in purity, understanding, patience
and kindness; in the Holy Spirit and in sincere love; in
truthful speech and in the power of God; with weapons
of righteousness in the right hand and in the left; through
glory and dishonor, bad report and good report; genuine,
yet regarded as impostors; known, yet regarded as
unknown; dying, and yet we live on; beaten, and yet not
killed; sorrowful, yet always rejoicing; poor, yet making
many rich; having nothing, and yet possessing everything.
(2 Cor. 6:3–10)*

*Whatever anyone else dares to boast about—I am
speaking as a fool—I also dare to boast about. Are they
Hebrews? So am I. Are they Israelites? So am I. Are they
Abraham's descendants? So am I. Are they servants
of Christ? (I am out of my mind to talk like this.) I am
more. I have worked much harder, been in prison more
frequently, been flogged more severely, and been exposed
to death again and again. Five times I received from the
Jews the forty lashes minus one. Three times I was beaten
with rods, once I was pelted with stones, three times I
was shipwrecked, I spent a night and a day in the open
sea, I have been constantly on the move. I have been in*

*danger from rivers, in danger from bandits, in danger
from my own people, in danger from Gentiles; in danger
in the city, in danger in the country, in danger at sea; and
in danger from false believers. I have labored and toiled
and have often gone without sleep; I have known hunger
and thirst and have often gone without food; I have been
cold and naked. Besides everything else, I face daily the
pressure of my concern for all the churches. Who is weak,
and I do not feel weak? Who is led into sin, and I do not
inwardly burn?*

*If I must boast, I will boast of the things that show
my weakness. The God and Father of the Lord Jesus, who
is to be praised forever, knows that I am not lying. In
Damascus the governor under King Aretas had the city
of the Damascenes guarded in order to arrest me. But I
was lowered in a basket from a window in the wall and
slipped through his hands. (2 Cor. 11:21–33)*

*I must go on boasting. Although there is nothing to be
gained, I will go on to visions and revelations from the
Lord. I know a man in Christ who fourteen years ago
was caught up to the third heaven. Whether it was in the
body or out of the body I do not know—God knows. And
I know that this man—whether in the body or apart from
the body I do not know, but God knows—was caught up
to paradise and heard inexpressible things, things that
no one is permitted to tell. I will boast about someone
like that, but I will not boast about myself, except about
my weaknesses. Even if I should choose to boast, I would
not be a fool, because I would be speaking the truth. But I
refrain, so no one will think more of me than is warranted
by what I do or say, or because of these surpassingly great
revelations. Therefore, in order to keep me from becoming*

*conceited, I was given a thorn in my flesh, a messenger
of Satan, to torment me. Three times I pleaded with the
Lord to take it away from me. But he said to me, "My
grace is sufficient for you, for my power is made perfect in
weakness." Therefore I will boast all the more gladly about
my weaknesses, so that Christ's power may rest on me.
That is why, for Christ's sake, I delight in weaknesses, in
insults, in hardships, in persecutions, in difficulties. For
when I am weak, then I am strong. (2 Cor. 12:1–10)*

In these autobiographical sections, Paul doesn't defend
himself by saying, "You've underestimated me. I'm really much
more impressive than you imagined." No. He basically responds
by admitting that they'd nailed his deficiencies. (Ironically, he
admits that he isn't rhetorically polished—and his response is
rhetorically polished!) He pleads guilty to all charges. He is a
broken vessel, weak and powerless.

Instead of spending his time working his way up through the
Roman world of honor and tribute, he was pouring out his life for a
cause he believed in. So he "commends" himself in a most uncom-
mendable way!

When it comes down to a biosketch, what's important is that he
follows the one who gave his life on a cross for others. The ultimate
problem isn't that the Corinthians underappreciated Paul; it's rather
that they misunderstood the heart of the Christian message—a
message that ends not with a Conquering Warrior storming the
gates of Jerusalem but with a crucified messiah who is hanging on
a cross outside the gates of Jerusalem. Paul, like the one he follows,
is broken and bruised, yet God is working in him.

This is the narrative context for Paul's famous "jars of clay" statement: "But we have this treasure in jars of clay to show that this all-surpassing power is from God and not from us."

It's not unusual today to hear ministers introduced by all their credentials: places where they've received degrees, honors they've been given, books and articles they've published—along with the mandatory statement that they're in demand all over the country. Blah, blah, blah.

Paul's convictions and his understanding of the story of Jesus didn't permit that perspective, however. He'd learned this secret: "When I am weak, then I am strong." That explains why he could say: "Therefore I will boast all the more gladly about my weaknesses, so that Christ's power may rest on me. That is why, for Christ's sake, I delight in weaknesses, in insults, in hardships, in persecutions, in difficulties."[2]

I mentioned in the introduction that I'm thankful for all the training I received in languages, in homiletics, in exegesis, in theology, and in practical ministry.

But my true teacher was Megan. She was, indeed, a jar of clay. She was broken and frail. Her only full sentence was, "I'm Megan!"

Of course, it was a sentence she'd say all day long. It's like she knew she'd only be alive for a few years, and so she didn't waste time sleeping. She'd be awake about twenty-two hours a day. To keep her from wandering around the house and even trying to go outside, Diane and I would take turns through the night sleeping with her. As I think back now, it was a funny (though groggy) scene: I'd have my arms wrapped around her to make sure she didn't get up, she'd get right up in my face so that I could feel her breath, and she'd shout, "Hey, I'm Megan!"

I'd say, "I know! Could you be quiet and let's get a little sleep."

Megan has been "asleep" in God's care quite a while now, but I'm still stunned that her life altered the world. This frail child. Just a jar of clay—broken and chipped. Mental disability, physical handicap, brief life—but still a witness to the story of Jesus, filled with love.

In addition to all her other challenges, Megan had a little limp. She'd limp around the house, limp around church, limp in the yard, limp in the street, while she'd sing her favorite song: "I may never . . ."—that's all she could get out, and then she'd fast forward to—"Yes, sir!"

And Megan's emphasis on "I may never" was accurate. As the song goes, "I may never . . . march in the infantry, ride in the cavalry, shoot the artillery." On and on she would sing endlessly. The two phrases she actually sang were "I may never" and "Yes, sir" (with appropriate salute and a big, crooked grin).

She didn't care about what others battled over; she would never carry a torch for power and performance, but she was a jar of clay filled with treasure, secrets that only after many years I've been able to identify and decipher.

A year after her death, several friends had a memorial celebration. They used various gifts—music, art, writing—to mark the richness Megan had brought into their lives. Thom Lemmons, remembering her love for the "I'm in the Lord's Army" song, wrote these words about "limping along in the Lord's army":

It's a strange regiment, this "Lord's army" of which she loved to sing. Its recruits, rank upon rank, are, every one of them, hurt and defective in some way. It's an army of the walking wounded, commanded by a general with punctured hands and feet and a gash in his side; a general who leads his host not to attack, but to surrender. And with this, we may be coming close to the center of Megan's meaning for us: her infirmity, her heroic, dogged struggle, and her eventual defeat reminded us, her comrades-in-arms, of our own concealed injuries.

As we watched her die, as we gathered around her grave, we all peered into ourselves and saw our own mortality, knowing ours was far more well-deserved. Having given her into the hands of the angels, we turned again to the fray, more acutely conscious of our own liabilities for the cause, our own poor choices, our own inherited blemishes, our own private defeats.

As Thom (and the others) noted, Megan was an embodiment of the kind of life envisioned by Saint Francis of Assisi:

Lord, make me an instrument of your peace.
Where there is hatred, let me sow love.
Where there is injury, pardon.
Where there is doubt, faith.
Where there is despair, hope.
Where there is darkness, light.
Where there is sadness, joy.
O Divine Master, grant that I may not so much seek to be consoled, as to console;
to be understood, as to understand;
to be loved, as to love.
For it is in giving that we receive.

It is in pardoning that we are pardoned,
and it is in dying that we are born to Eternal Life.
Amen.

One of my treasures is a Willie Mays baseball card. He and Mickey Mantle were my childhood heroes. I guess the card is worth a good bit—I don't know exactly how much. The card is in very good shape, and to preserve it, I have it in a little plastic sleeve that I probably paid a dime for.

Imagine seeing me show this card to someone and having him respond, "Wow! That is a beautiful plastic jacket!"

I'd reply, "No, not the jacket, the card inside—"

"No, no, that is a beautiful plastic sleeve," the person says. "The way the corners are perfect, no fingerprints to speak of—that's an incredible plastic jacket!"

I would think, "You are missing it. The treasure is in there—my Willie Mays card! Don't become obsessed with the packaging."

And if you said to Paul, "Your bio is not that impressive. Your life is broken," Paul would say, "You're absolutely right."

Perhaps he'd even wink and add, "It's broken more than you can imagine."

But inside there's a treasure!

My guess is that some who are reading feel like their spiritual resume has been rejected—because of divorce, depression, loss, mistakes, or inabilities. As the old spiritual says: You cannot sing like angels; you cannot preach like Paul. (Ironic, isn't it? The problem in Corinth is that they weren't that impressed with Paul's preaching!)

But there is power in that humble awareness. Weak is the new strong. It's the "secret," the message that fits our cruciform gospel. As we follow the one who was crucified in weakness, we experience the deep mystery that Paul had discovered: "When I am weak, then I am strong."

Which makes me think: my daughter had Olympian strength. She had heavyweight strength in a super flyweight body!

Despite her handicaps and challenges—despite the fact that the world would look at her exterior and see a broken vessel, an inferior resume—Megan knew what was truly important. She knew "I'm Megan!" God had used this broken jar of clay to create a beautiful person, one who would show so many people the love of God through the glory of the imperfect. Megan needed no other resume than that, and neither did Paul. It was one of Megan's greatest gifts that she could know so completely and intuitively what it takes most of us a lifetime to grasp.

6

The Power of the Powerless

It is hard to believe that God would reveal his divine presence to us in the self-emptying, humble way of the man from Nazareth. So much in me seeks influence, power, success, and popularity. But the way of Jesus is the way of hiddenness, powerlessness, and littleness. It does not seem a very appealing way. Yet when I enter into true, deep communion with Jesus I will find that it is this small way that leads to real peace and joy.[1]

—Henri Nouwen

One of the great qualities of Alcoholics Anonymous is the first pillar of the program: "We admitted we were powerless."

Sometimes it takes hitting rock bottom in addiction or selfish behavior or the experience of losing a close family member or friend to recognize how powerless we really are over our lives—to understand how fragile life is.

For many of us, success and the illusion of control keep us from realizing how powerless we really are. This is not a challenge for people with disabilities, who already know that life is not about accidents of birth, beauty, or performance.

In Christopher de Vinck's incredible book, *The Power of the Powerless*, he writes about his mentally handicapped brother: "Oliver still remains the most hopeless human being I ever met, the weakest human being I ever met, and yet he was one of the most powerful human beings I ever met."

Trust me: those words strike me as rock-solid truth.

He tells about two girls he brought home with him during his dating years.

When I was in my early twenties I met a girl and I fell in love. After a few months I brought her home for dinner to meet my family.

After the introductions, the small talk, my mother went to the kitchen to check the meal, and I asked the girl, "Would you like to see Oliver?" for I had, of course, told her about my brother.

"No," she answered. She did not want to see him. It was as if she slapped me in the face, yet I just said something polite and walked to the dining room.

Soon after, I met Roe, Rosemary, a dark-haired, dark-eyed, lovely girl. She asked me the names of my brothers and sisters. She bought me a copy of The Little Prince. *She loved children. I thought she was wonderful.*

I brought her home after a few months to meet my family. The introductions. The small talk. We ate dinner; then it was time for me to feed Oliver.

I walked into the kitchen, reached for the red bowl and the egg and the cereal and the milk and the banana and prepared Oliver's meal. Then, I remember, I sheepishly asked Roe if she'd like to come upstairs and see Oliver. "Sure," she said, and up the stairs we went.

I sat at Oliver's bedside as Roe stood and watched over my shoulder. I gave him his first spoonful, his second. "Can I do that?" Roe asked. "Can I do that?" she asked with ease, with freedom, with compassion, so I gave her the bowl, and she fed Oliver one spoonful at a time.

The power of the powerless. Which girl would you marry? Today Roe and I have three children.[2]

When my son Matt got married, Diane and I talked about how we wished Megan could have known her sister-in-law, Jenna. Megan would have loved her. And Jenna—trust me—would have been like Roe, the second woman in de Vinck's story. Here's the letter I wrote to Megan not long after their wedding:

My Dear Megan,

Last week when I was looking for your old percussor, Mom said, "It may be in Megan's toy box." Without thinking, I began digging through the box, and then it overwhelmed me. I was immersed in you: your shoes, a couple of your favorite blouses, the stuffed cat you loved, etc. I could smell you, hear you, even feel you there.

All that to say that I've never stopped missing you. It's been about ten years; but in grief-years it's been so much less in some ways and so much more in other ways.

You rocked my world, my precious daughter. You didn't enter this world with a bright intellect like your brothers did. You were, we eventually learned, "mentally handicapped."

Big deal. There were so many other ways in which you were so precocious: in love, in forgiveness, and in joy.

The only full sentence I ever heard you say in ten years was "I'm Megan"—and yet you became my minister who led me further along the way of Christ. Without even intending to, you exposed the shallowness of this world—a world obsessed with externals.

You were a jar of clay.

It's hard to picture you at the age you'd be now. You have remained ten in our minds.

Since you died, life has in some ways been easier. You never wasted much of your short time sleeping! Easier . . . yet sadder. We would gladly go without sleep to be able to hold you and sing with you. ("I may never march in the infantry. . . .'; "This is a song that doesn't end. . . .'; "Jesus loves me. . . .")

We would have loved seeing your joy at Matt and Jenna's wedding. (You never got to meet her, but I think she would be your best friend.) And I imagined you there in ICU patting Christopher's broken and bruised body after his wreck.

Your simple faith still guides us. Your love overwhelms and empowers us.

Soon and very soon, my dear. . . .

Love,
Dad

A strange kind of power—power that can hardly be communicated to our competition-fueled culture—flows out of de Vinck's moving account of his blind, mute, crippled, retarded, helpless brother. Henri Nouwen's foreword captures some of the impact:

When I finished reading The Power of the Powerless *I had a strange vision. I saw our crazy world, full of wars*

*and conflicts, full of competition and ambition, full of
heroes and stars, full of success stories, horror stories, love
stories and death stories, full of newspapers, television,
radios and computer screens, and millions of people
believing that something was happening that they
couldn't miss without losing out on life. And then I saw
a hand moving this heavy curtain of spectacles away
and pointing to a handicapped child, a poor beggar, a
chronically ill woman, an illiterate monk, a dying old
man, a hungry child. I had not noticed them before. They
seemed hidden so far away from where "it" seemed to be
happening. But the hand pointed gently to these poor,
humble, weak people and a voice said, "Because of them
I won't let this world be destroyed. They are my favored
ones and with them I made my covenant and I will be
faithful to it."[3]*

The power of the powerless. I can't tell you how many times I've
heard similar words from parents of children who are mentally handicapped, who are autistic, or who have some other learning disability.
As challenging as that life can be, the parents are forced to receive
a different reality—one that seems crazy and out of control in the
beginning but that can begin to look amazingly honest and refresh-
ingly sane after a while (though still difficult much of the time!).

Christian ministry begins by accepting the relationship God
has created with God's people—weak, frail, broken, sinful people—
through the faithful life and death of Jesus Christ.

NEBUCHADNEZZAR, INC.

This deep reliance on God—the true mark of spirituality!—runs
counter to our desire for the kind of power that people so often crave.

In the Old Testament story of Daniel, one man thought he had all the power, and his craving for more was insatiable. King Nebuchadnezzar of Babylon had it all! He was powerful enough that today he might be called "Nebuchadnezzar, Inc." Fresh from a great military victory at Carchemish over the Egyptians (605 BC), he was maybe the most secure man in the universe. Youth, strength, wealth, clout—all were his! He was a steel tank, a shining knight, a superhero.

Besides all that, his name was impressive. As one third grade girl once wrote to me: "Dear Mr. Cope, I discovered that Nebuchadnezzar is more than half the alphabet. That's fourteen letters. Love, Elizabeth." Good point—he had that going for him, too!

But every night, when the king put his head on his royal pillow, he became as vulnerable as the lowliest peasant in Babylon. And it was then that God struck! The chink in his armor is revealed in these three words: "Nebuchadnezzar had dreams."[4]

In his dream stood an enormous, dazzling statue with a head of gold, chest and arms of silver, belly and thighs of bronze, legs of iron, and feet of iron and clay. What an imposing reminder of the power he had, this King Golden Head (for the head represented him), and of the power subsequent kingdoms would have.

Did Daniel, Shadrach, Meshach, Abednego, or any of the other exiles need a reminder that he held all the trump cards? They'd seen his domination in Jerusalem, and they'd heard of how his Chaldean kingdom had conquered peoples all around the Fertile Crescent.

But there's more to the dream: a rock cut out of a mountain strikes the statue and smashes it to pieces. It doesn't just destroy the feet (representing the final kingdom); rather, it demolishes the whole statue.

This rock is the kingdom of God. And that's exactly what this rock has done—again and again! The rule of God enters human history, and it overwhelms the power-hungry kingdoms of humans. It happened during the time of Daniel. This pagan king had numerous opportunities to humbly confess the power and deliverance of God.[5] It happened a generation later when God worked through Cyrus to return the covenant people to Israel. It happened again when the Jews faced the persecutions of Antiochus Epiphanes, and many resisted the urge to adjust, adapt, and follow all the rules.

But it happened supremely in the ministry, death, and resurrection of Jesus Christ. The people with all the fame and power—Caesar Augustus, Herod the Great, Archelaus, Antipas, Caesar Tiberius, Pontius Pilate—were no match for this one who was "meek and humble in heart." Through his righteous life and death, the kingdom of God broke in with power and force.

During this time when the values of the kingdom come into such sharp contrast with the values of this world, a time when the kingdom has arrived but not in its fullness, God's people continue praying, "Thy kingdom come, thy will be done on earth as it is in heaven."

The most countercultural thing the church can do is to continue praying "Thy kingdom come, thy will be done." For this rock (the reign of God) has come and smashed the strongholds of this earth. And it continues beating away.

SHARON: The Deeper Power of Gratitude

Through Jesus, we have come to redefine what true power looks like. In the lives of people we know, we experience this kingdom value being lived out. In vivid contrast to Nebuchadnezzar, Inc.

are two people I know who embody the values of the kingdom and stand in relief against the false front our culture has propped up by mere illusions of power.

One Sunday, I spoke about the countercultural values that the kingdom of God calls for. I gave the example of the poor widow in Mark's Gospel standing in stark contrast to the way Nebuchadnezzar came to know power.

> *Jesus sat down opposite the place where the offerings were put and watched the crowd putting their money into the temple treasury. Many rich people threw in large amounts. But a poor widow came and put in two very small copper coins, worth only a few cents. Calling his disciples to him, Jesus said, "Truly I tell you, this poor widow has put more into the treasury than all the others. They all gave out of their wealth; but she, out of her poverty, put in everything—all she had to live on." (Mark 12:41–44)*

Jesus witnessed the widow generously dropping her only two copper coins into the offering at the temple. But how do we receive a story like that? How can we—amid all our resources and the desperate needs of the world—respond? Most of us have become numb to such a radical sacrifice.

But shortly after I finished speaking, the real sermon for the day began. It was preached by a young, mentally disabled woman on row two.

As the weekly offering was taken, Sharon began scouring through her purse, desperately searching for something to give. But there was nothing. Not one coin.

Several of us near her then saw her feeling her pockets, desperately wanting to give generously, like the woman Jesus had commended. When all else failed, she popped a bracelet off her wrist and dropped it in the collection plate.

Someone later gave me the bracelet and suggested that I return it to her. "It isn't worth anything," he explained.

On one level, that was true. This bracelet didn't come from Tiffany's. It didn't even come from QVC or from the jewelry counter at Wal-Mart. It couldn't have been worth a dollar. But she didn't know that! It was gold-colored, and to her it was twenty-four-carat. She gave all she had.

So instead of giving the bracelet back to her, I decided to keep it and tell people about it. Since then, I've shown her bracelet to tens of thousands of people. It has become a sacrifice more precious than gold in its encouragement to so many others.

KENNETH: The Deep Power of Encouragement

On another Sunday, when I was nearly lost in grief and discouragement, I looked at a line of people waiting to visit me. I was exhausted from preaching and from grief, and I didn't know if I had the energy for the conversations to come.

Then I saw Kenneth, a mentally disabled member of our church, who'd come to the front of the line. He bellowed loudly, "Hey, Mike. I just read this in the Bible and wanted to read it to you. 'How beautiful are the feet of those who bring good news.' I just thought you might like to know that."

Then he disappeared as quickly as he had appeared.

Years have passed since Kenneth read those words to me, but they still carry a tremendous power in my life. Kenneth didn't have "PhD" or "Inc." behind his name, or a staff or a posse, but his words stood out that day more than any other conversation I had. Kenneth expressed the values of the kingdom in his urgency and terse words unclouded by comment.

God used him that day to lift me up—and Kenneth's gift, like the widow's mite, was valuable beyond measure because it was given in love.

HIDDEN POWER

Where does power reside in this world? The values of God's world indicate that the true dynamos of the kingdom are people like Sharon and Kenneth, in their actions and words that carry the gospel message in power. As Nouwen says, these who live the "small way" of Christ—the often unappealing way of hiddenness, powerlessness, littleness—are the most powerful humans on the earth.

When Megan died, she didn't leave much behind—at least not much that would bring a handsome sale price on eBay. But what she did leave is electrifyingly powerful.

There's her cat. That little stuffed cat that she carried through the day and slept with at night. She cared for it like it was real. She petted it. She sucked on its paw and tail. Even now when I pick it up, my mind thinks I can smell her and hear her and experience her compassion.

There's her ribbon and bell. We often had Megan wear what we euphemistically called her "special necklace"—which was really some ribbon with a bell tied at the bottom so we could try to keep track of her movements. She was often on the go, day or night. (She was a constant door-checker, always looking for the possibility that someone forgot to lock a door so that she could go exploring. My parents' house still has dead bolts up high on nearly every door in the house—which always takes some explaining when people notice them. It was their attempt to keep her where they knew she was safe.)

I'm sure that some probably saw Megan, like the widow in Jesus' story, as a drain on society's resources; yet, through her, God gave so much to the world and to those who knew her. Even though she didn't leave behind much of worth from this world's perspective, she left behind another gift: power. The power of a Christ-shaped life.

A power that I feel every day.

7

The Ex-Demoniac's Testimony

In my experience those richest in faith are those who have endured great pain.[1]

—Darryl Tippens

Over and over again, Scripture shows weak people as the strong witnesses to the power and steadfast love of God.

As I read Mark 5:1–20 recently, it struck me that the story called for a testimony. That is, after all, what Jesus asked from the man who'd been healed. "Go home to your own people and tell them how much the Lord has done for you, and how he has had mercy on you."

This is the man who becomes, in the words of N. T. Wright, "the first apostle to the Gentiles"—finding a new life and telling in Gentile areas what Jesus had done for him.

I began by asking why the man was living at a cemetery; in that question, I imagined some overlap with my own story. I have spent a lot of time at that tiny little plot of ground just southwest of Abilene where Megan is buried.

I remember hating how cold and rainy it was on the day of her funeral. As a minister, I'd been to cemeteries scores of times before to pray, to read scripture, to comfort loved ones. I'd done so in every imaginable weather: snow, ice, rain, sweltering heat, strong winds. But this time, I resented the weather conditions: I didn't want that ground to be wet—not the ground in which my daughter's body had been lowered.

For the first year or two, I'd slip out of the office whenever I could to go sit there and remember. At one level, I know it doesn't make sense. Megan is dead, and I'm really no closer to her there than anyplace else.

But I also believe in the Celtic concept of "thin places"—spots where the distance from heaven to earth seems particularly thin and translucent.

So here's his own account of what happened to that man in Mark 5 (as I envision it).

THE TESTIMONY

Most people can't imagine moving to a cemetery. But I didn't move there. Not really. I migrated there. I guess I just found myself there more and more. At first, when my daughter died, I just visited there. But over time, my life back in Damascus seemed futile. People wanted me to get on with my life. "You'll have other children," they assured me. They told me that people have to get over their grief and press ahead, letting time do its work. And then that tomb on the eastern bank of the Sea of Galilee—well, that started to seem more real than my home in Damascus. It felt like I was guarding my little girl, like I was refusing to leave her in her suffering. I didn't *want* my grief to end because that felt like the end of memories of her laughter. And her crying.

So at some point, I just left home. The cemetery of the Gerasenes became my new home. And there, in the vast expanse of my grief, the door to my soul was left ajar.

And like the legions of Roman soldiers that kept marching unwanted into our region, another Legion entered my heart. To put it bluntly, hell came goose-stepping into my life.

Almost immediately, I couldn't tell where I ended and the demons began. They tormented me. They deluded me. They drove me to despair.

I became an animal, prowling around the nooks and crannies of those hills. I've heard tales since then of how I frightened all the mothers of the Ten Cities. They warned their children never to stray near the Gerasenes.

They warned about a bedeviled lunatic who was naked, who cut himself with stones, and who would cry out day and night. It sounded like urban legend, but this one checked out. It was true. I was your worst nightmare.

A few times, the mothers shoved the fathers out the door with their weapons and their chains to come bind me to protect their families. But nothing that could chain me was as powerful as the evil that was in me.

I came to these tombs to lament my daughter's death. Now I couldn't wait for my own death. I begged these unclean spirits to let me pass.

And then one day . . . I looked out on the lake and a boat was coming. They apparently didn't know about the madman that people were supposed to avoid.

When they saw me, I expected to see the quickest about-face in history. But one of the Jews got out of the boat and began walking toward me. I'm still astounded. He was a Jewish teacher; I was an unclean man in an unclean place with an unclean crowd of demons stirring inside.

When I saw him, I ran, I sprinted, and then I fell, pleading with him to remove my suffering. That voice that bellowed from inside me screamed: *"What do you want with me, Jesus, Son of the Most High God? In God's name don't torture me!"*

This Jesus looked at me—without fear and without repulsion—and he asked, "What is your name?"

That voice that overwhelmed me answered, *"My name is Legion. For we are many."* Then that voice—the voice of these unclean spirits—began begging him not to send them out of the area. *"Send us among the pigs. Allow us to go into them."*

Then, in an instant, hell's demons fled. I watched in amazement as two thousand pigs stampeded off a steep bank into the lake.

The last thing I saw was the people who tended the pigs running in all directions, undoubtedly to tell people what had happened. No doubt they were frightened—and a bit upset about their livelihood.

While they were running, while chaos was breaking out all around . . . I was sane. For the first time in a long time. "So this is what sanity feels like," I thought to myself. I'd pretty much forgotten. I did the one thing that made the most sense. I got dressed.

With each garment of clothing I slipped on over my scar-ridden body, I realized how naked my life had been.

I couldn't wait to see some of the people who'd known me as a scary madman. They'd be overjoyed to see my good fortune.

Or so I thought. Because when they came back, there were the same, familiar looks etched on their faces. Sheer fear. I guess anything they couldn't explain frightened them. As a man who couldn't get past his grief, I frightened them. As a Legion-possessed, self-mutilating, naked lunatic, I frightened them. And now, as a man who'd been healed, I scared them as well.

They begged Jesus to leave. And I begged to go with him. "This will be wonderful," I thought. "I'll follow him wherever he goes. He'll never leave my sight."

And then perhaps the most perplexing part of all happened. He told me I wasn't going with him. "Go home to your own people," he said. "Go back and tell them how much the Lord has done for you."

He didn't tell me to enter the priesthood. He didn't tell me to preach the good news around the world. He simply asked me to go home, to return to the Decapolis, and to report on what had happened to me.

Which is just what I've been doing. No big fanfare. No book deals. No TV appearances. I'm just telling people what the Lord has done for me.

Let the weak say I am strong.
Let the poor say I am rich.
Let the blind say I can see.
It's what the Lord has done in me.

8

Minister, Equipper, Friend, Confessor

If the world is sane, then Jesus is mad as a hatter and the Last Supper is the Mad Tea Party. The world says, Mind your own business, and Jesus says, There is no such thing as your own business. The world says, Follow the wisest course and be a success, and Jesus says, Follow me and be crucified. The world says, Drive carefully—the life you save may be your own—and Jesus says, Whoever would save his life will lose it, and whoever loses his life for my sake will find it. The world says, Law and order, and Jesus says, Love. The world says, Get and Jesus says, Give. In terms of the world's sanity, Jesus is crazy as a coot, and anybody who thinks he can follow him without being a little crazy too is laboring less under a cross than under a delusion.[1]

—Frederick Buechner

Who would have imagined that a handicapped girl could have been such a remarkable witness of God's steadfast love and grace? Yet I know four people who believe she *was* the incarnation of the second secret: weak is the new strong.

Even in her most vulnerable moments of suffering, Megan was a minister, equipper, friend, and confessor to these four individuals who told me their stories and kept me breathing when I thought I would never breathe again.

THE LAWYER

Two weeks after Megan's death, when the world was a black hole, when people who still had a life were getting back to it, when I couldn't breathe . . . a six-page, handwritten note came from a young attorney in Arkansas.

He told me how his life had been driven by greed and power. His supreme goal in life had been to become a partner by the age of thirty-five.

He reflected on how we had met, on the hours we spent talking, on the big issues of life that we had discussed.

But then he told me that the real conversion of his life came from meeting and getting to know Megan. She aspired to nothing but love. She had no enemies. He said that through her he learned the meaning of Paul's words: "[We are] sorrowful, yet always rejoicing; poor, yet making many rich; having nothing, and yet possessing everything."[2] He'd also come to learn the truth of the beatitudes with their upside-down world: "Blessed are the poor in spirit . . . blessed are the meek . . . blessed are the pure in heart. . . ."

Then this young attorney told me that while I had been his pastor and friend, my frail, mentally handicapped daughter had been his minister. She had challenged his materialism, his anger, his hunger for power, his lack of concern for others. What many others had tried to say in words she had communicated to him in wordless weakness, and his life had been changed forever.

THE MISSIONARY

The day after Megan died, a fax arrived from a young missionary in Uganda who said he'd give anything if he could make it home to honor her by being at the funeral. But since he couldn't be there, he wanted Diane and me to know that Megan had changed his life. In the message, he said:

> *Medical people may have called her handicapped, but looking deep into Megan's beautiful eyes made us all wonder who the handicapped in this world really are. She was shortchanged in quantity of life, but I hope that no one dares eulogize her as being shortchanged in quality of life. She had life, and she had it abundantly . . . so abundantly, in fact, that she left a little behind for each of us. She lives on in our hearts and deep in our souls.*

Mark was part of a group of college students who came to our house every week. And there at our house, he said, he was loved without condition and without limit by Megan. He recalled how she would crawl up on his lap, burying her head in his chest. Then she'd pound her chest and yell, "I'm Megan!"—followed by a start-up attempt at "I'm in the Lord's Army" or "Jesus Loves Me."

Now he and his wife were part of a team of young families planting churches in the rural villages of southeast Uganda, and he wanted us to know that she had been a vital part of the team. She had equipped them in ways that no one else was prepared to do.

A child who'd never travelled much had become part of a team of missionaries in Africa, traveling inside their hearts to take the love of God into all the world.

THE OLD MAN

Just an hour before Megan took her last breath, the oldest man in our church came into her pediatric ICU room to say "good-bye." He actually stretched the truth a wee bit to get in, telling the nurses that he was her great-grandfather. In an extended, metaphorical sense, that was true.

Even now I tear up as I try to think of words to describe how much John and Megan loved each other. Megan loved to hold John's aged hands; and he loved to buy her elegant dresses. She may have been the nicest-dressed child at our church (if you saw her before she began peeling things off), thanks to the generosity of this former clothes salesman.

He walked into our holy space, placed a hand on her head, raised the other hand, looked up, and said, "May the gates of heaven open wide to receive this sweet child." His words are carved into my memory.

Here was the perspective of one who loved so much, who knew that death isn't final, who understood that a well-lived life was coming to an end. His final act of friendship was a great-grandfatherly blessing just before Megan died.

THE CONFESSANT

Two days before Megan died, another special friend of Megan's came in to see her. He asked if he could have a minute alone.

"Alan" had been one of her favorites. From the moment she met this kindhearted man, she felt at home in his arms.

It wasn't until much later that I learned Alan had asked to see Megan alone because he had been carrying a secret for many, many years. Something he felt he could tell no other human being.

So for the first time in his life, in the presence of pure love in human flesh, he shared the deepest secret of his life. When he told me about it, he said that he still trembled as he remembered the look of understanding and love in her eyes.

"Well, she didn't understand," you might say.

I don't know. There were just too many stories like this in her life. She wasn't precocious with logarithms or history, but she was brilliant when it came to compassion and understanding.

THE BRUISED REED

Why would an attorney speak about Megan as his minister? Why would a missionary point to her as his equipper for ministry? Why would an old man find such an attachment to her? Why would a man with so many friends share the deepest secret of his life with this ten year old?

My suspicion is that this takes us to the deepest meaning of God's world—a world of true shalom. In most human experience, power and competition keep us at a safe distance from each other.

But there came one whom the prophets had spoken about:

He had no beauty or majesty to attract us to him,
nothing in his appearance that we should desire him.
He was despised and rejected by others,
a man of suffering, and familiar with pain.

Like one from whom people hide their faces
 he was despised, and we held him in low esteem.
Surely he took up our pain
 and bore our suffering,
 yet we considered him punished by God,
 stricken by him, and afflicted.
But he was pierced for our transgressions,
 he was crushed for our iniquities;
 the punishment that brought us peace was on him,
 and by his wounds we are healed.
We all, like sheep, have gone astray,
 each of us has turned to our own way;
 and the Lord has laid on him
 the iniquity of us all.
He was oppressed and afflicted,
 yet he did not open his mouth;
 he was led like a lamb to the slaughter,
 and as a sheep before its shearers is silent,
 so he did not open his mouth.
By oppression and judgment he was taken away.
Yet who of his generation protested?
For he was cut off from the land of the living;
 for the transgression of my people he was punished.
(Isa. 53:2–8)

He was a bruised reed. This one was born into the powerful world of Caesar Augustus, yet in a tiny corner to a cast of unknowns. While people all around the Roman world were searching for connections and recognition, he grew up simply and humbly.

One of his followers, perhaps echoing a song of the early church, put it like this:

Who, being in very nature God,
did not consider equality with God something to be
used to his own advantage;
rather, he made himself nothing
by taking the very nature of a servant,
being made in human likeness.
And being found in appearance as a man,
he humbled himself
by becoming obedient to death—
even death on a cross!
Therefore God exalted him to the highest place
and gave him the name that is above every name,
that at the name of Jesus every knee should bow,
in heaven and on earth and under the earth,
and every tongue acknowledge that Jesus Christ is Lord,
to the glory of God the Father. (Phil. 2:6–11)

Why would someone make his or her confession to Megan?

Let me ask you: Who would you rather tell—someone who seems to have it all together or someone who will look at you with undiluted love?

This is the second secret: weak is the new strong. Jesus honored those who are often invisible in our world: the meek, the mourners, the poor, the hungry and thirsty. As Philip Yancey noted, "Jesus was the first world leader to inaugurate a kingdom with a heroic role for losers."[3]

God promised to humble the proud and to raise up the humble. In Megan he did just that: he raised up this one who was weak and unassuming to be his minister of reconciliation to all around her.

Third Secret

Life Together Is
Our Only Hope

A blizzard does more for community than all the modems on earth....Connection to others is the great generator of meaning in life. When we are without deep attachments, our lives skim along the surface.[1]
—David Wolpe

So often we try to get on with the life of faith as if we were hermits, struggling on our own. Perhaps we are too proud to admit that we need help; more likely, we have simply failed to realize that others are accompanying us. Every step of the long kingdom road has been graced by the presence of others before us and moistened with their tears, whether of joy or sorrow. We may learn from what they have already experienced, just as we may find reassurance in the knowledge that they have been through the wildernesses of this world before us. We may take comfort from the presence of others who even now are making that journey alongside us.[2]
—Alister McGrath

9

Intubated by Friends

There is a Jewish custom, se'udat havra'ah, the meal of replenishment, which is practiced during the period of mourning after the death of a loved one. After returning from the cemetery, the mourner is not supposed to serve others or take food for herself. Other people feed her, symbolizing the way the community nourishes and sustains the mourner in her grief. Solidarity with the pain is the beginning of the healing, Henri Nouwen has said.[1]

—Darryl Tippens

One fear I had in writing this book was knowing that I'd have to go back into the early, numbing years of grief. Sure enough—I found page after page I'd written with words like these: *I'm a zombie pastor. People think I'm living, but I'm dead. I keep going through the motions of ministry, but inside I'm shell-shocked, numb, lifeless.*

These words of John Claypool express what I felt many days as I stood before a congregation to preach:

Please do not expect any great homiletical masterpiece.
Do not look for any tightly reasoned, original creation.
Rather, see me this morning as your burdened and broken
brother, limping back into the family circle to tell you
something of what I learned out there in the darkness.
The first thing I have to share may surprise you a bit, but
I must in all honesty confess it, and that is: I have found
no answers to the deepest questions of this experience [his
daughter's cancer and then later her death].[2]

I was descending into the icy ocean depths with poor visibility, and I felt like my depth gauge was broken. When I tried to come up for air, I couldn't find the hole in the thick ice on the surface. I cried out to God, *How much deeper will I fall, O God?* When my precious daughter died, I felt like someone was stepping on my chest, and there was no way to get the boot off my chest. How would I have recognized a heart attack if I had one? How would I ever find joy again in my life?

My walk was a terrible and painful limp. No, I couldn't even call it a walk most of the time in those months following Megan's death. It was a feeble crawl. I struggled to breathe. I journaled: *I'm in a dark hole. I don't know how deep it is. Or if it gets even deeper. Or if it is ever possible to get out. I can't breathe. My friends have been my ventilator.*

As I looked through these old passages I'd written, I kept coming across some version of this theme: "My friends have been my ventilator." They were breathing for me. They shared my grief, they didn't hold expectations for me to "get over it," yet they slowly invited me to life in this new, post-Megan world.

It was something Megan had taught me. My tendency, in pride, is to think I can make it on my own, Lone Rangerish. But Megan didn't have that pride. She had welcomed people into her caring community—doctors and nurses, friends and strangers, grandparents and children. Though she couldn't express all her thoughts with words, her kind eyes and her patting hands made it clear: I need your help, and I'm so thankful that you care. (Ironically, everyone who ever cared for her testified that they had received much more from Megan than they'd ever given to her.)

It was a lesson we desperately needed. That wasn't the last time we'd brush against death; nor was it the last time we desperately needed our friends to breathe for us.

THE WRECK

It had been just over a decade since Megan died. We had, at least in some ways, survived.

That's when I went to our church building to pick up my (then) sixth grade son, Chris. He'd been with about a hundred other middle schoolers and high schoolers from our church to an event in the Dallas area.

I watched as one after another of the SUVs pulled in. I saw kids pouring out of eleven vehicles, bleary eyed and exhausted. But where was the twelfth vehicle?

I saw Sarah, our brand-new youth minister in the hallway, and I asked her if everyone was back. I could see her fighting back tears, and she shook her head no.

"Is something wrong? Was the other in a wreck?" I asked. She shook her head yes.

"Is Chris in that one?" The dam holding back tears burst, and she nodded yes. I quickly pieced together from a few people—including someone on a cell phone at the wreck scene—what had happened.

An SUV with one adult, two eighth grade girls, and five sixth grade boys had been in a single-car accident on I-20 just outside Putnam, Texas. I remember hearing: the wreck is serious . . . helicopters are on the way . . . parents should go to the ER at Hendrick Hospital and wait.

I was numb. *Not again. We can't do it again.* I walked up to a classroom where Diane was meeting with some middle school girls and broke the news to her.

"Is he alive?"

"No one could say."

We huddled in a family waiting area at the ER with people who would later become dear friends. Two highway patrolmen showed up and asked to meet with one of the couples to break the news that their son was dead. My whole life I'll remember Jennifer's maternal cry.

Soon, Dr. Jim Morrison, a good friend of mine and an ER doctor, came to get us. He tried hard to smile and said, "He's okay. He's beaten up pretty badly. But I think he's okay. We're about to run tests."

He led us back to a room where Chris was lying, beaten almost beyond recognition. They couldn't get a response from him; apparently he was in shock.

When he heard our voices, he began crying uncontrollably (even as I am now as I write this). I leaned over and whispered into his bloody ear the words I'd said to him at bedtime thousands of times:

> *Love that boy.*
> *Like a rabbit loves to run,*
> *I said I love that boy.*
> *Like a rabbit loves to run.*
> *Love to see him in the morning.*
> *Love to say, "Good mornin', son."*[3]

With those words, he calmed down a bit. My prayers for the previous hour had been fairly simple: "Please, God. Please, God. Please, God. Please, God." I think you'd expect more from a forty-eight-year-old minister. But that's all that would come.

As I leaned over him, not yet knowing how serious his internal injuries were, nothing profound came. So I prayed the same words I'd said for many years over the babies born at our church: "May the grace of the Lord Jesus Christ, the love of God, and the fellowship of the Holy Spirit be on you always."

The doctors decided to intubate Chris and fly him to Cook Children's Hospital in Fort Worth, and they told us that one parent could go with him in the helicopter. I was smart enough to know not even to suggest that I should be that parent—Diane's quick glance suggested that it wasn't even a remote possibility!—so I ran home, grabbed some clothes, dropped a note on my blog asking for prayers, and headed to Fort Worth. (In the following few hours, people from six continents left notes on the blog saying they were praying for us. We never heard from the pagans in Antarctica.)

DOWN IN THE DITCH

As I look back now, I realize that we survived the wreck because of intubation. Not just the breathing assistance Chris received from physicians—but the breathing done for us by friends when we couldn't breathe for fear, the praying done for us when we were too tired to pray.

It was the same way we'd survived the death of Megan. It's how we survive all of life's disappointments and losses.

The first to pray were already praying before I even knew there was a wreck. Seven middle school boys from our church in the vehicle behind the wreck were told by the driver—as he got out to go help—to stay in the car, and they began praying immediately for their friends. They prayed when we, the parents, didn't know to pray.

There were also the many people all over the world, as the comments on my blog from January 16, 2005, attest, who carried us in prayer and encouragement. When we were frozen by fear and could hardly think or speak, others offered those prayers.

We found as the weeks and months of recovery began that our friendship with the families of the other children in the wreck was life-giving. We knew each other's scars. We grieved with Brody's parents. We celebrated as children got out of wheelchairs. We offered encouragement when infection kept striking one of the boys who had suffered broken bones in both legs.

And we thanked another "community" who had taken care of our children and the driver when we couldn't. Before we even knew about the wreck, a community of strangers who happened to be traveling on I-20 that Sunday afternoon jumped down into the ditch to hold our children.

One complete stranger held Brody while he was dying; another, a woman from Monahans, held our son and tried to keep him warm and awake.

Later, someone admitted to me how embarrassed he was that he'd been on I-20 that day and was just mad about the traffic that was backed up for miles and hours. He got teary-eyed and said, "I had no idea."

Of course he didn't. I've been in the same position.

But the people who did see—the ones who knew there were wounded little bodies littering the ditch—these "Good Samaritans" ran into the ditch and took care of them.

About six weeks after the wreck, when we were dismissed from the hospital and I was preaching again, I invited the eight families from the wreck down front. It was an emotional sight to see everyone up there—two in wheelchairs and one on crutches, Brody's parents and brothers, and all the rest of us.

Then four from the group—two children and two parents—offered testimonies about what they'd learned about friendship and community.

Here is what Diane said:

When I first heard the news that my child was in a serious car accident, I could hardly bear the fact that he was somewhere alone, hurt, and afraid, and I wasn't there. Then a couple of days later, I heard news about those who helped our children. I can't begin to tell you how comforting that was for me.

In this world where people are afraid to get involved,
our children were surrounded by warm, caring adults.
As a mother, I am especially thankful for the women who
were whispering into our children's ears with their calm,
soothing voices. I'm thankful that they took our places
in the dirt, since we couldn't be there. And I'm grateful
that they held our children's hands and provided their
mothering touch.

On that cold Sunday afternoon in January, these
women and men became community in a way I'll
never forget.

After her words, we invited down to the front many of those who had stopped to help the wreck victims as they lay injured that afternoon. We had invited all we knew of, many of whom our families had been in contact with by phone to thank—people from New Mexico, Monahans, Midland, Lubbock, and Abilene. Can you imagine what it was like for us to see them in person for the first time?

Then we invited down all the emergency response people who were able to come. We had thirteen or fourteen of them there, and once they were all down front, the church broke into long standing ovations at both morning assemblies.

These people who stopped to hold Brody as he was dying and to care for the other seven as they were cold and frightened are a living witness to this old text:

Two are better than one,
because they have a good return for their labor:
If they fall down,
they can help each other up.

But pity those who fall
and have no one to help them up!
Also, if two lie down together, they will keep warm.
But how can one keep warm alone?
Though one may be overpowered,
two can defend themselves.
A cord of three strands is not quickly broken.
(Eccles. 4:9–12)

WHY ARE YOU CRYING?

The year after the wreck, during the previews before a movie, Chris glanced over at me and saw big, fat tears falling off my face. He asked, "Hey, Dad, why are you crying?"

To Chris, no preview could justify those tears—unless they were tears of joy for the unexpected release of another *Bourne* or *Lord of the Rings* movie.

I gave him a short, brush-off answer. It wasn't the time or place.

But what I wanted to say was:

Because we're here. In the dark. In this theater. And you're sitting next to me.

Because you could have died a year ago.

Because I can still hear your mom sobbing, "O God, please not again."

Because you were beaten beyond recognition. Because we heard the Bourlands crying out in the hospital when they were told that Brody had died. Because I can still remember those nights in ICU at Cook's with the Bennetts and the Lemmonses.

Because I held my breath for forty-eight hours, waiting to see if you'd breathe on your own.

But also because you're all right. Because you didn't have to stay in that wheelchair or that back brace. Because I saw you play football this fall, and because you're playing point guard now. Because you're an incredible young man who is loved by your peers and by all younger kids. Because we're back to wrestling. Because the five of us got to hike all over the mountains of Colorado this summer.

And because I can lose to you every day in a game of P-I-G.

Because of how close we feel to the other families impacted by the wreck.

Because of our spiritual family all around the world who prayed for you and the others. Because I can still feel your brother's hug when we met at Cook's after he flew from Houston and I drove from Abilene. Because I still remember Jenna's tears as she cared tenderly for you—her brother-in-law for only seven months at the time. Because Dr. Jim loaded up and drove to Fort Worth to watch over the three of you and your families himself (while letting those ER docs do their jobs). Because one of our elders, a physical therapist, came over to hold you steady while you showered and carefully bind back up your wounds. Because another of our elders, a teacher at your middle school at the time, met you each morning to help you up and down the stairs in your wheelchair.

Because there's no better sight for me than seeing you and your brother playing together—catch or basketball or PlayStation—when he's home.

Because we were not alone in the pit. Others were breathing for us when we were suffocating, praying for us when we couldn't.

And because sometimes my grief gets confused, and I still cry about Megan.

That's what I wanted to say, but I didn't. No seventh grader wants to hear that with a bag of popcorn and a great sports movie coming on.

10

Known by the Scars

Very slowly, the immediate agony subsides. Around the edges of that opening, things begin to heal. Scar tissue forms. The hole remains, but instead of allowing only a constant stream of emptying, it begins to permit things to enter. We receive some of the love and wisdom that loss has to give us. Now is when loss can have content beyond the ache. This is the time to create meaning. Pay attention to what comes in that open space. Nothing can make the pain go away. Making loss meaningful is not making loss disappear. The loss endures, and time will not change that truth. But now it has some purpose.[1]

—David Wolpe

We'd much rather be impressively intact than broken. But only broken people share spiritual community.[2]

—Larry Crabb

We all wear scars. Some are visible on the skin. Others aren't as easy to see but are just as real.

Nicholas Wolterstorff, following the unexpected death of his son in a mountain climbing accident, wrote: "The wounds of Christ are his identity. They tell us who he is. He did not lose them. They went down into the grave with him and they came up with him—visible, tangible, palpable. Rising did not remove them. He who broke the bonds of death kept his wounds."[3]

As the risen Christ said to Thomas, "Put your hand in my wounds, and you will know who I am," so Wolterstorff says, "I bear the wounds of his death. My rising does not remove them. They mark me. If you want to know who I am, put your hand in."

Scars mark our identity. In Homer's *The Odyssey*, the Trojan War is long past. Odysseus has been away from home for twenty years, and finally he's back in Ithaca, but everything is a mess. Because so many people thought he wasn't coming back, all the suitors are there for Penelope and for his property. In order to know what's happening, Odysseus disguises himself as a beggar and goes among them. Nobody can tell who he is except for his old nurse because she sees a scar on his leg that was familiar to her. She remembered when he got the scar hunting boars as a boy.

Like Thomas with the resurrected Jesus, the old nurse recognized Odysseus by his scars.

Not only do scars show identity, but scars very often have a story to tell.

In the movie *Jaws*, there's a great scene in which the crusty old captain and the cocky marine biologist have a one-upmanship contest comparing who has the worst scars. They're pulling back sleeves and yanking up pants legs, pointing to scars and telling about danger and close calls with death. Each time one of the characters reveals a scar, there's a story that goes with it.

You could give somebody a bit of a tour of your life by describing scars.

I could show you my smallpox vaccination scar. Many of us have them because, as recently as 1967, two million people died of smallpox. Those scars mark the fact that the disease has been eradicated. So I bear that reminder of how epidemiologists traveled with vaccines worldwide trying to lasso that horrible disease.

I could show you a scar on my shoulder from the time I was twelve years old in Missouri. One day I was riding my bike when some crazy driver got in my way as I ran a stop sign. I escaped with my life, but today I still bear that scar that tells a story of a carefree—or is it careless?—boy on a Schwinn one summer day.

For a few years, I bore a scar from the top of my right shoulder all the way down past my waist on the left side because I broke a basic rule of scuba diving when I was coming up: I neglected to look where I was going. I swam up under a man-of-war, whose tentacles caught me across my (shirtless) chest. I thought I'd had a heart attack. I bore that scar for a long time before it faded.

My older son bears a scar that takes us back to the week after Megan died. Matt was twelve at the time and was wrestling with his two-year-old brother on the floor. It was all in fun, but Chris knew he was outmatched. He reached around and bit off the lower part of one earlobe. Diane, who had raised Megan and was not shaken by anything, picked up the earlobe, put it in a bag, and went to the emergency room. It was one of those "sew it back on and ask questions later" visits to the ER!

The feat earned Chris a place of respect among his older brother's middle school friends, who started calling him Mike Tyson.

Many years have passed, and the scar is not obvious, but it's still a reminder: don't mess with your two-year-old brother.

Most of us have scars that tell stories. They are reminders of childbirths, of battles, of accidents, of surgeries, of pain.

Annie Dillard tells of an Algonquian woman and her baby who were left alone after everyone else starved during a brutal winter.

The woman walked from the camp where everyone had died, and found at a lake a cache. The cache contained one small fishhook. It was simple to rig a line, but she had no bait, and no hope of bait. The baby cried. She took a knife and cut a strip from her own thigh. She fished with the worm of her own flesh and caught a jackfish; she fed the child and herself. Of course she saved the fish gut for bait. She lived alone at the lake, on fish, until spring, when she walked out again and found people.

Those scars have whole stories behind them. That scar she bore on her thigh told the story of how she'd saved the life of her child.

Near the end of his letter to the Galatians, Paul says: "From now on, let no one cause me trouble, for I bear on my body the marks of Jesus."[5]

It's not hard to imagine that Paul's torso bore scar-upon-scar-upon-scar that were reminders of the times he'd been stoned, shipwrecked, and flogged.

And now, he says to the Galatian believers, he bears "the marks of Jesus"—the *stigmata* (the Greek word Paul uses that means "scars" or "marks" and that later came to refer to pain people felt as they experienced the wounds of Jesus from his crucifixion).

COMMUNITY AND SCARS

I've thought many times since Megan's death about what Wolterstorff said: if you want to know me, you have to know something about my wounds, my marks, my scars. And, of course, the opposite is true: if I want to truly know you, I must know about your deepest wounds. There can be very little genuine friendship until we are willing to know each other's scars.

I have a friendship that began just a few years ago with a guy who never knew Megan. When we were getting to know each other, the first thing he said was, "Tell me about Megan. I wish I'd known her." In that request, he was asking to hear my story, willing to look on the scars that her death has left.

But it's difficult for us—we are fearful of what others will think if we reveal our deepest emotional scars. Will they be horrified at such wounds?

I have talked to several people who have found their most trusted community in recovery groups for that reason. Wounds and scars are expected there. You can be honest about your struggles, your failures, and your wounds without fearing an onslaught of shame. It is a shame-free zone.

But what would happen if we took our friendships deeper by sharing these scars from grief and loss? For the scars tell not only about our wounds but also about the healing that has begun to take place (if, indeed, it has).

We desperately need people who will know us and love us as we are—while encouraging us as we inch forward as God's people. We need those who will listen without getting tired, who will offer perspective on our lives, and who will remind us that we are more than the sum total of our scars.

For we are not just our wounds. We are much more than our shortcomings and our failings. In full, open, honest friendship, we are reminded of that!

11

The Christmas Quarter

*The worst days now are holidays: Thanksgiving,
Christmas, Easter, Pentecost, birthdays, weddings,
January 31—days meant as festivals of happiness and joy
now are days of tears. The gap is too great between day
and heart. Days of routine I can manage; no songs are
expected. But how am I to sing in this desolate land, when
there's always one too few?*[1]

—Nicholas Wolterstorff

actually got to meet Dr. Channing Barrett, though I don't remember the meeting because I was too young. But that doesn't change my picture of him as a young man walking a marathon of miles every weekend. In my mind, I see him returning home to Blissfield, Michigan, around the turn of the century.

Channing Barrett was one of eight boys and was the first in the Barrett family to go to college. From his medical school, he walked twenty-five miles home each weekend, always returning a couple of days later with clean clothes, a food packet, and a dollar.

Dr. Barrett became one of the first ob-gyns in Chicago, practicing at Cook County Hospital. He was widely known both for his innovative surgical techniques and for his ambidextrous skills that allowed him to change hands during long procedures.

There was no patient he wouldn't accept. He delivered many "tenement babies" for fifty cents and many babies for the wives of Mafia dons for a good bit more!

With a growing, respected medical practice, a wonderful wife, and three children, this young physician seemed to be living the idyllic life. He enjoyed riding horses and lifting weights, and he was an early member of the Polar Bear Society—that "unique" group that takes to the chilly waters of Lake Michigan in January each year to prove—well, who knows what they're trying to prove?

And then World War I interrupted this Norman Rockwell life. Dr. Barrett left Chicago to run a field hospital in France, followed shortly by his seventeen-year-old son, who fought in the trenches.

As long as he could, Barrett sent money back to his wife and daughters. But by the last year of the war, his funds were nearly exhausted. He had no more to mail home. Mrs. Barrett sold most of what they owned, trying desperately to keep her daughters fed and clothed without having to sell their house.

By the time Christmas rolled around in 1918, there were no presents to place under the tree. They were lucky to have a place to live.

But Mrs. Barrett had managed, despite all the financial scrimping, to save two quarters. So on Christmas morning, when the girls emptied their stockings, under the paper dolls their mother had cut out for them and under a few pieces of candy, they each found a coin.

Previous Christmas mornings had been more lavish, filled with frilly dresses and expensive toys. And there would be more such mornings in the future. But this was the Christmas the family would always remember.

For that Christmas and every future Christmas—even after things turned around after the war and they received gifts—when the girls emptied their stockings, they always found—under the apples, oranges, nuts, and candy—a quarter.

It was a reminder—a reminder that some years are good, while others aren't too good. Some years deliver new babies, promotions, raises, and great promises. Other years offer sickness, failure, death, and deep disappointment.

The quarter reminded them about both possibilities. It warned them not to write off all the pain of the past as if it didn't exist. It taught them that the sorrows and wounds of their lives had shaped their characters as much as their joys and accomplishments.

Anyone who takes seriously the Christmas stories of Scripture knows that the first Christmas had more than angels, shepherds, wise men, and a mother nursing her baby. There was also the anguish of childbirth. There were the pungent, impolite odors of an animal pen.

There was an old man who held the baby and told his mother, "A sword will pierce your own soul too." There were the voices of many mothers screaming for their baby boys being slaughtered by a demented ruler named Herod. There was a breathless escape to

Egypt as Mary and Joseph sought to protect their child, who was the true "Prince of Egypt."

The entrance of God's Son into the world meant peace—but it didn't ensure that people would get along. It meant great joy—but it didn't mean we'd always get to grin. And it meant unconditional love—though it never implied that everyone would act lovingly.

And so one family, year after year, continued dropping a quarter of remembrance into the bottom of each child's stocking.

At least one of Channing Barrett's children picked up that tradition. Every year through the thirties, forties, and fifties, her five children, Dr. Barrett's grandchildren, pulled their stockings off the chimney on Christmas morning to find quarters buried under fruit, nuts, and candy.

And at least one of those five passed it on to her four children. And at least one of those four is passing it on to his children.

The quarter has mysteriously tied this family together—binding even generations who never met. Together they have remembered that bad year in 1918 and other bad years since.

One year brought the safe birth of a new nephew; another brought the self-inflicted death of a relative who couldn't keep fighting the demons of his life.

One year brought the thrilling news from the gynecologist that a baby was on the way; another brought the news from the pediatrician that the baby wasn't developing right.

Some years brought joy; others brought deep, deep pain. The quarter is a remembrance that the meaning of Christmas is deeper than our triumphs and sorrows. It is a joy that can't fully be expressed, a peace that passes understanding.

For years, my children have followed this tradition started by their great-great-grandmother Barrett. Together, we've experienced the love of God, woven through the fabric of good days and dark days.

Many Christmases ago, the quarter represented a burden that was crushing our hearts. It wasn't long before the Christmas of 1994 that Megan took her last breath. While her stocking still hung on our chimney that Christmas morning, its presence proclaimed her absence.

Megan's death was surely the darkest moment of our lives.

We felt very connected to Matthew's Christmas story, the one that tells of "Rachel weeping for her children."[2]

And several Christmases later, our family returned to that grief when my brother's son, Jantsen Barrett Cope, died suddenly and unexpectedly after lifting weights with his high school football team. I had no idea how we'd all gather in my parents' living room without his big, joyful laughs. Fifteen is too young to die.

Our quarters that Christmas were quarters of grief.

And yet, life has moved on—with grief and joy walking hand in hand. My wife, Diane, put it well in a Communion meditation she recently presented at our church just before Christmas:

Christmas is coming! This time of year holds different emotions for many people depending upon their life circumstances. It's changed for me through the years, as well. As I let my mind drift back over my own past, a stream of words and ideas came to me, representing how the meaning of Christmas has changed for me during my lifetime: Santa, presents, joy, anticipation,

*giving, receiving, excitement, snowflakes, songs, jingle
bells, hot chocolate, caroling, ornaments, Christmas
trees, pine smells, Jesus, baby, angels, shepherds, manger,
anticipation, fake Christmas trees (I'm married to a man
allergic to pine), gift giving, stress, parties, exhaustion,
more stress, darkness, deep sadness, aching from the
soul, Jesus' birth but also his resurrection, emptiness,
suffocation, tears, family, giving and receiving, love, hugs,
the joy of children.*

    *Sixteen years ago on November 21, I lost my daughter.
She died at the age of ten. Many of you knew Megan. You
held her, laughed with her, sang with her. Many of you
didn't get the chance to let Megan change your world,
and she would have! Megan was mentally challenged
and medically fragile. I watched her suffer for at least
two years before her death. She died a few days before
Thanksgiving. So, since then, my Thanksgivings and
Christmases have never been the same. Each year since
that terrible one, I have had to fight through the holidays,
pretending to enjoy the holidays for my own children and
extended family, making myself just walk through the
expected celebrations. I never wanted it to be that way,
but it has just been hard.*

    *Then, on November 15th of this year, our second
granddaughter was born, Ellie. How wonderful to have
something good happen during this time of year. She has
brought joy and light in the midst of dark memories.
God has used her and her big sister, Reese, to change my
feelings about this time of year. And my joy is somehow
richer and more complete because I came to it through
darkness and pain.*

    *I couldn't help but realize that Ellie's birth was
similar to Jesus' entrance into the world. As Ellie has*

brought me joy in the midst of sadness and pain, making this time precious to me again, Jesus entered a world full of darkness, pain, and despair, and we have celebrated his birth ever since. This beautiful newborn baby, Jesus, God in this child, brought forth light into the darkness. He created a new hope for his people. He has created new hope for all of us. And our joy is made complete because we have come to it through the pain of separation from him.

So, as we share this Communion today, let us be reminded of the love of God. That he used the birth of his son to help open our eyes to the joys and sorrows of this world. That as God allows us to walk through the darkness in order to come to joy, so may we walk beside others as they go through the darkness. That as he sent light into the darkness, so may we bring his light to each other. That as he sent love and joy to others, so may we also provide love and joy.

As Christmases continue to come around, our family will pass this old tradition along. These quarters remind us that by God's grace we have survived, and that hanging together through joy and sorrow is our only hope of survival.

12

The Left Hand of Fellowship

I have a son who was born without a left hand. One day in Sunday school the teacher was talking with the children about the church. To illustrate her point she folded her hands together and said, "Here's the church, here's the steeple; open the doors and see all the people." She asked the class to do it along with her—obviously not thinking about my son's inability to pull this exercise off. Yet in the next moment it dawned on her that my son could not join in. Before she could do anything about it, the little boy next to my son, a friend of his from the time they were babies, reached out his left hand and said, "Let's do it together." The two boys proceeded to join their hands together to make the church and the steeple. This hand exercise should never be done again by an individual because the church is not a collection of individuals, but the one body of Christ.[1]

—Randy Frazee

We all need the kind of "left hand" that Frazee describes.

I remember a kind of comedic "left hand" my younger son had when he was two: his ten-year-old (but mentally disabled) sister.

127

Even then, he could figure some things out that she couldn't—like where the Cheerios stash was kept. He knew—but he couldn't reach it. One day I watched him lead her into the kitchen and point to the shelf. She reached up, grabbed them, and handed them to him. He slung them all over the kitchen floor, where they could pick them up for a little snack.

A tragic event like "the Wreck" brings a community together, but I want to take this idea one step further. Neighbors can come together for short periods of time around tragedy, but something must continue to sustain them. What is it that sustains us when life seems wrecked—when damage is irreversible?

The important secret that life with Megan taught me is that only in community can we find what sustains us for the long haul. Rugged individualism won't cut it, given life's vicissitudes and disappointments.

In job interviews, there are many hopes and dreams, some- times promises or agreements that don't pan out. But even before we moved to Abilene two decades ago, someone made a commit- ment to Diane that became a reality which will forever bond us with the Highland Church. During the interview process, one of the elders (John Willis) told Diane, "If you move here, we'll help raise Megan."

When we returned home from that interview, I heard sounds of packing from the other room. Diane said, "You take your time and make your decision. The kids and I are moving to Abilene."

Diane knew what I've come to know over twenty years: we cannot make it alone. We need friendships that go to the bone. We need a left hand.

A PLACE OF BLESSING

Spiritual friendships are critical because they provide the blessing
we need in this hurting world to remember that we are loved and
valuable—despite our failures and wounds.

A friend of Henri Nouwen's, a wonderful woman who was
mentally disabled, came to him asking for a blessing. So he walked
up to her and made the sign of the cross on her forehead.

"Henri, it doesn't work," she objected. She needed more. So after
the service, he said, "Janet wants a blessing." Here's what happened:

*I had an alb on and a long robe with long sleeves. Janet
walked up to me and said, "I want to be blessed." She put
her head against my chest and I spontaneously put my
arms around her, held her, and looked right into her eyes
and said, "Blessed are you, Janet. You know how much
we love you. You know how important you are. You know
what a good woman you are."*

*She looked at me and said, "Yes, yes, yes, I know."
I suddenly saw all sorts of energy coming back to her.
She seemed to be relieved from the feeling of depression
because suddenly she realized again that she was blessed.
She went back to her place and immediately other people
said, "I want that kind of blessing, too."*

*The people kept walking up to me and I suddenly
found myself embracing people. I remember that after
that, one of the people in our community who assists the
handicapped, a strong guy, a football player, said, "Henri,
can I have a blessing, too?" I remember our standing there
in front of each other and I said, "John," and I put my
hand on his shoulder, "you are blessed. You are a good
person. God loves you. We love you. You are important."*[2]

One evening, our little covenant group decided we would bless all the children of our group at the beginning of the school year. Each adult wrote and read a blessing for a child who wasn't their own. All these many years later, I can still hear the words of Mary as she poured out words of affirmation and love to Megan—thanking her for her simple joy.

In a world where we tend to be evaluated by wins and losses, by financial portfolios, and by status, such friendships remind us that our worth is much deeper and much more secure.

A PLACE OF SENDING OUT

It's also in these friendships that we can call each other to lives that are larger than our disappointments. We can remind each other that we were made to join God in his work of restoration. We encourage each other to remember that, though we may be broken, we have been called to seek God, as Dietrich Bonhoeffer suggested, in "the neighbor who is within reach."

Short of this centrifugal perspective that launches us into God's world, we can wind up obsessing on our pain. But as we move outward in compassion and justice with our friends, neighbors, and strangers, we're invited to move beyond that pain. The pain itself might, in fact, uniquely "qualify" us for deep connections with others.

My father expected to spend his final decades doing the things he loves: jogging (he'd run the Boston Marathon five times), playing with his grandchildren and great-grandchildren, hiking, traveling, etc. But those plans were altered when he was diagnosed with Parkinson's disease.

The first year of dealing with the disease was so difficult because he had to face all the disappointments that go with it. But he soon began making decisions that would prevent the disease from taking away his joy. So much of his waning energy is spent serving other people—at their church, in our family, around their community.

A PLACE OF LIFE-SUPPORT

It had been a wonderful family getaway to the lake over Memorial Day weekend in 2007 for Tod and Lee Ann Brown and their four children: Bailey, Hutton, Connor, and Reagan. But on the way back to Midland, Texas, they were in a tragic accident that claimed the life of their thirteen-year-old son, Connor.

When I saw them, I recognized the numbness and the grief from my own experience with loss. Lee Ann described her grief eloquently a few weeks after the accident:

As for me . . . I am heartbroken. I never knew the meaning of that before and now I do. There are times I can go for a few hours and just do normal things . . . but then the incredible wave hits me, and I'm completely under the grief again. The other day I started sobbing . . . not a quiet, polite sob but a loud and ugly sob . . . the kind that would scare the people around you. I needed to and it felt right, but I didn't want Reagan or Bailey to have to witness it, so I went into the laundry room. I just got in the corner and let go. After a minute I felt a hand on my shoulder. Reagan had come in, and he just sat down on the floor and hugged me. He didn't ask me to stop; he just sat with me. There are many moments like this during my day.

About the same time, Tod wrote: "I have decided that grief is more like a dance than a journey. There are steps forward and backward and side to side. It doesn't really seem like there is progress, just moving around a dark room in different directions. The song is slow and sad. I wish there were more choreographed steps to the dance."

Then he returned to describing the grief a couple of weeks later:

Grief is a burdensome weight that won't be laid down. Like a demanding child, it must be carried. It just won't go away. Years ago, I very nearly severed my left index finger. It became gruesomely infected and was the most physical pain of my life. For the first couple of weeks, my finger never left my conscious thought. It throbbed so badly I could feel every heartbeat. Then came the phase where it wasn't in my conscious thought, but if I bumped into something, pain would stab through my body. I was very careful with it. Now, years later, it is scarred and feels different because the nerves are damaged. But I don't think about it every second, and it doesn't hurt in ways that incapacitate me. I think that is how healing works.

In the tradition of biblical faith, the Browns refused to pretend. They expressed their sadness and their belief in words of lament and hope—such as in this "Lament for Connor" (July 17, 2007; Tod Brown):

*That ugly scar of fresh turned earth
Holds tight my broken son whose worth
The world will never know. And I
Turn stricken face to steely sky*

And ask a question that will start
Fresh groaning from a broken heart.

Where were you, God, on that dark road
When violence took what I adored
And crushed him? Did you see her shock,
Her wailing, kissing bloody locks?
Did you stand by with folded arm
Or with your finger cause this harm?

What did I do to make you mad?
If this is love I've more than had
Enough. How can I speak of you
To foes when this is what you do
To friends? I'm worn out now and just
Begun to walk the path I must.

Yet I have nowhere left to turn
For hope or joy. I cannot learn
Another voice than first I knew
And trusted. Were they true,
The promises you made to me?
Can I full trust what I can't see?

I know that my Redeemer lives.
I know a Sovereign takes and gives.
I am a blind and broken man,
So I will hold on while I can
For now. Is grace enough to keep?
Until we see your face, I weep.

These words of protest, questioning, and trust ring true with some of the most eloquent expressions of faith in Scripture. Some don't want to hear them, which is why we've at times performed what

Eugene Peterson described as a *psalmectomy*—excising those Psalms that don't seem faith-filled enough for our delicate tastes.

If you ask Lee Ann and Tod how they've survived these past few years, they won't point you to some mysterious "healing of time" but to the concrete love and support of their community of friends. They'll tell of people who cried with them . . . people who took immediate action after Connor's death to do things like sit with his body at the funeral home while they were tending to their injured daughter . . . friends who continue telling stories about Connor, who acknowledge his birthday every year (as a way of saying, "We haven't forgotten!"), and who let them be sad when they are.

Even early on, Tod recognized the place of these deep soul-friendships:

> *I am deeply grateful for friends this morning. Grief is a black hole. It threatens to suck you into yourself. There is a part of me that wants to pull away from everyone and everything. It would be easy to crawl into bed, pull the covers over my head, and just disengage. But it is lonely there. And we have friends . . . who gently refuse to let us drift off into isolation. With tenacity and patience, they have stayed with us. Early on, there was unvoiced skepticism in my heart that when the shock receded, the promises of care and concern would fade into good intentions. I was wrong. There is a friend who sticks. I don't know what we would do without you all. We are experiencing a love that will not let us go. I think that kind of love lies buried under the surface of life and is only really revealed to a broken heart.*

The Browns have discovered what Diane and I learned through pain: that while everyone needs deep friendships, those of us who have raised children with special challenges or who have suffered great loss cannot live without them. These friends are the left hand of fellowship with whom we learn to applaud—through joys and sorrows.

13

The Way of Grief

Sometimes grief looks like narcolepsy.[1]

—Anne Lamott

Every great loss demands that we choose life again.
We need to grieve in order to do this. The pain we have
not grieved over will always stand between us and life.
When we don't grieve, a part of us becomes caught in the
past. . . . Grieving is not about forgetting. Grieving allows
us to heal, to remember with love rather than pain. It is
a sorting process. One by one you let go of the things that
are gone and you mourn for them. One by one you take
hold of the things that have become a part of who you are
and build again.[2]

—Rachel Naomi Remen

t's early, early on Christmas morning as I write this chapter. I'm thinking about my favorite word from all the Christmases when the children were little: preassembled.

I have my earbuds in listening to Handel's *Messiah*, remembering his exclamation after twenty-two days of inspired composing:

"I did think I did see all Heaven before me, and the Great God Himself."

And I'm pondering those words embedded in Matthew's Christmas story: "Rachel weeping for her children and refusing to be comforted, because they are no more."[3]

Who was this Rachel, and why did she seem to be the symbol of grief during the slaughtering of infants in Matthew?

THE SOUTH SIDE OF THE JABBOK

Genesis 32 zooms in on the northern bank of the Jabbok River where Jacob wrestled with a man throughout the night. The "man" wrenched Jacob's hip and changed his name to Israel. Meanwhile, Rachel and her children—and the other women and their children—waited for Jacob to cross the Jabbok.

So that's where I imagine her—on the south side of the Jabbok, waiting for Jacob.

She sat on the banks of the Jabbok, allowing the wind whipping down the canyon walls to slowly dry her damp hair. It had been quite a chore getting the whole clan of Jacob across the Jabbok River. All the clan, that is, except her husband, Jacob.

She was a bit envious of him, knowing that he'd have a quiet night alone on the other side of the river. An evening of peace and quiet, no loud children of the co-wives. He'd probably come bouncing into camp the next morning.

She thought back to when she'd first met him. She had taken her father's sheep to the well for watering. An older man—someone who looked like his fortieth birthday was in the rearview mirror—approached her, explained he was a cousin.

He turned out to be a kissing cousin. And crying cousin. He kissed her and broke out into tears.

Stunned, she ran back to her father, Laban, and told him what had happened. Jacob stayed and worked for her father, and after a month, Laban wanted to know what wages he wanted.

Jacob was in love with his *much* younger cousin. So he said he'd work seven years for her—years that would seem like only a few days.

The wedding day came, and at the last moment, her father took the wedding veil off her and put it on her older sister, Leah. "I can't marry away my younger daughter first," Laban thought. He said it would disgrace Leah.

So a few days later there was another wedding.

Rachel remembered how difficult it was to get pregnant. The goal was to have children—especially sons—for her husband. But she couldn't get pregnant. And yet there were babies everywhere.

That is, after the baby wars began. It all started when Leah gave birth to four sons in a row. Leah 4 – Rachel 0. So Rachel gave her servant Bilhah to Jacob. Then Leah gave *her* servant to Jacob.

Leah gave birth to Rueben, Simeon, Levi, and Judah.

Bilhah gave birth to Dan and Naphtali.

Zilpah gave birth to Gad and Asher.

Leah gave birth to Issachar and Zebulun.

Rachel? Still no sons.

Rachel's hair was nearly dry as she looked back over the Jabbok to where Jacob was camped. She recalled how Reuben had found some mandrakes, which were thought to work like fertility drugs. So she traded Leah one of her own nights with Jacob for the mandrakes.

Finally, she got pregnant and gave birth to a son, and she said, "God has taken away my disgrace." She named the son "May he add another"—*Joseph*.

One day, word had come from Jacob to pack everything up quickly. They were leaving Haran. She stole her father's household gods—small idols. Why? Maybe for a bit of home, but more likely it was a concern for the future, and she thought the gods might help.

When they had crossed the Euphrates River, Laban tracked their traveling group down and was livid about the gods being stolen. He went into her tent to find them, but she'd put them in a saddlebag and was sitting on it, claiming that she was having her period and didn't feel like getting up.

The men made peace. Her father kissed her and the others and returned to Haran. Now they were returning to Paddan Aram where she would meet her brother-in-law, Esau, for the first time. She'd heard plenty of stories about him. Jacob's description had put the image in her mind of a hairy animal. He was ruddy, hairy, and from the way Jacob told it, he wasn't the brightest lamp on the wall. Worse, he likely would be very bitter, angry enough to send warring parties out to meet them.

Why does Jacob want to put his whole family at risk all to make peace with his brother? She wondered what was ahead for them, if anything but destruction.

She got up and walked back to camp, and her husband soon arrived, having forded the Jabbok.

Jacob came into camp less perky than she thought he might. He looked like he hadn't had a very restful night. He looked like he'd been wrestling all night, not sleeping.

He told them to line up for meeting Esau: Bilhah and Zilpah would be first in the procession, followed by Leah, and then Rachel and Joseph would come last.

❀　❀　❀

Jacob's family traveled to Shechem, then to Bethel, where undoubtedly all the children heard the story of what had happened to their father there twenty years before.

They went to Bethlehem, a journey Rachel took while pregnant with her second son. But she had so much trouble while giving birth, she knew she would die. So she named the boy "Son of my trouble"—*Benjamin.*

And Rachel died in childbirth.

The book of Genesis gives a barebones description: "So Rachel died and was buried on the way to Ephrath (that is, Bethlehem). Over her tomb Jacob set up a pillar, and to this day that pillar marks Rachel's tomb."[4]

Later, the narrative says, Jacob told his son, Joseph, about his mother: "'As I was returning from Paddan, to my sorrow Rachel died in the land of Canaan while we were still on the way, a little distance from Ephrath. So I buried her there beside the road to Ephrath' (that is, Bethlehem)."[5]

That sounds like the end of it.

RACHEL'S WAIL THROUGH THE CENTURIES

But centuries later, the Lord says to the prophet Jeremiah:

> *"A voice is heard in Ramah,*
> *mourning and great weeping,*
> *Rachel weeping for her children*
> *and refusing to be comforted,*
> *because they are no more."*[6]

Like a grandma or a great-grandma, Rachel is weeping as she sees her children being forced into exile by the power-hungry Babylonians. She weeps on behalf of every other woman for the loss, for the disruption of life, for the sense of abandonment.

Those words are remembered by Matthew centuries later. Once again, Rachel, this wife of Jacob and one of the mothers of the nation Israel, is weeping. This time because little babies are being slaughtered in Bethlehem as a jealous madman named Herod kills anyone who might be a threat to his power. Irrational brutality.

Greg Boyd describes that horrific night like this:

> *On a cool fall night in Bethlehem, late in the 34th year*
> *of the reign of king Herod, a peasant family of five sleeps*
> *quietly in a one room shanty at the edge of town. They*
> *are startled awake as two Roman guards burst through*
> *their door shouting something about an edict from a*
> *king. The terrified couple sits up in their straw bed but*
> *are commanded to remain still by a soldier who holds his*
> *sword inches from the neck of the young mother. Nothing*
> *is said as the other solider holds his lantern up to each of*
> *the faces of the three frightened children, as if to inspect*
> *them. "How old is the boy?" the soldier sternly asks as he*
> *leans over the couple's youngest child. "He's not even two,"*

*the sobbing mother says with a quivering voice and a tone
that pleads for mercy.*

*The soldier suddenly rips the boy out of his tiny
bed with both hands and makes his way to the door.
The husband lurches toward the soldier but is knocked
unconscious by the blunt end of his comrade's sword. The
desperate mother manages to grab the leg of the soldier
carrying her son out the door, but he shakes her off and
then kicks her face. The woman cups her gushing nose,
forces herself off the floor and stumbles outside. Lying in
the path several yards from the house she sees her little
boy lying on the ground. She screams and falls to her
knees beside the boy. Blood is trickling out of his mouth.
He mutters something unintelligible as their eyes make
contact, for just a moment, one last time. Her boy had
been run through twice with a sword. She looks up at the
two soldiers who are quickly making their way down the
path to the next Bethlehem shanty. At the top of her lungs
she cries, "Why?"[7]*

These tears of Rachel are recalled by Herman Melville in *Moby
Dick*. Captain Ahab is approached by the captain of another whaler
who's desperate. While he was hunting whales, Moby Dick had
shown up. One of his smaller boats had harpooned the great whale
and been pulled off by it. Maybe the vessel had sunk, maybe it was
lost at sea.

The vessel was not just any small boat. That boat had held one
of his sons. He was desperately searching for him.

Ahab refuses to help. Melville says, "But by her still halting
course and winding, woeful way, you plainly saw that this ship that
so wept with spray, still remained without comfort. She was Rachel

weeping for her children, because they were not." Sadly, the vessel named "Rachel" turned away to continue the search.

In Genesis, Rachel is not buried in Hebron with her husband and relatives; rather, she's buried out there all alone. Lonely tomb, but alive in the Hebrew tradition.

She's there in the biblical witness: patron saint of all those who have lost a child, all those who've suffered greatly, all those who think God has forgotten them.

But the story is not finally about her alone, of course. This is wonderful, poetic language to say that God has not forgotten.

God was there on the banks of the Jabbok; God was there when Jacob buried his beloved; God was there when the children were taken by Nebuchadnezzar into exile; and God was there when all those baby boys were slaughtered in Bethlehem. The Lord was there and continues to be there, faithfully keeping the covenant.

GRIEF AS A GIFT

We live with grief. Life doesn't turn out the way we expect, and we suffer the loss. The health we expected into old age is suddenly lost. The child we thought was "normal" turns out to have special challenges. The teenager we love more than life makes destructive choices. The job we worked hard for is suddenly lost in a downsized economy. The marriage we thought was perfect turns out to be wearisome. The one we love so much dies. Rachel keeps weeping for her children.

The years roll by and grief changes. But it doesn't leave. And sometimes it sneaks up and bites us unexpectedly.

Long before I'd ever heard of Team Hoyt—Dick Hoyt and Rick, his son with cerebral palsy—Megan was my frequent companion as I trained for marathons. She loved the feel of the wind and the up-close view of the outdoors. As I ran and pushed, she clapped her hands, sang little bits of her favorite songs, and occasionally yelled, "Hey, I'm Megan!"

I didn't know how much I missed those running experiences together until ten or eleven years after her death. On the Sunday in August that our congregation is full of parents dropping off children at college, I took the stroller (which remains in an honored place in the garage) as a prop to talk about the challenge of letting go.

But in both services, the moment—the MOMENT!—I touched the stroller, I melted down. Through the years, I had some emotional moments while preaching. But never like this. The memories were just too strong.

What I've learned about grief, though, is this: it's the only way. I can't ignore it; I can't set it aside; I can't pretend. I must grieve my way through the sorrow and the loss. Painful as it is, grief is a gift—a part of the healing process.

It allows me to remember; it forces me to remember how strong love was and is; it slowly—slowly!—allows me to imagine a new future. And it keeps me dependent on God, eventually looking back over the many miles and realizing how true the words of the psalmist are: "You turned my wailing into dancing; you removed my sackcloth and clothed me with joy."[8] This is not a naive, Pollyannaish joy. This is the joy of those who have known deep loss, who have wept the tears of Rachel, who have lived in friendship with others who allow the balm of healing to slowly work (and who are themselves part of that balm of healing), who have been turned by God back to life in this desperate world, and who have learned to hope.

Fourth Secret

The End Is Not the End

It is hard to explain how this sunlit land was different from the old Narnia as it would be to tell you how the fruits of that country taste. Perhaps you will get some idea of it, if you think like this. You may have been in a room in which there was a window that looked out on a lovely bay of the sea or a green valley that wound away among mountains. And in the wall of that room opposite to the window there may have been a looking glass. And as you turned away from the window you suddenly caught sight of that sea or that valley, all over again, in the looking glass. And the sea in the mirror, or the valley in the mirror, were in one sense just the same as the real ones: yet at the same time they were somehow different—deeper, more wonderful, more like places in a story: in a story you have never heard but very much want to know. The difference between the old Narnia and the new Narnia was like that. The new one was a deeper country: every rock and flower and blade of grass looked as if it meant more. I can't describe it any better than that: if you ever get there, you will know what I mean.

It was the Unicorn who summed up what everyone was feeling. He stamped his right fore-hoof on the ground and neighed and then cried:

"I have come home at last! This is my real country! I belong here. This is the land I have been looking for all my life, though I never knew it till now. The reason why we loved the old Narnia is that it sometimes looked a little like this. Bree-hee-hee! Come further up, come further in!"[1]

—C. S. Lewis, *The Last Battle*

1 4

Not Yet

Waiting is not a very popular attitude. Waiting is not something that people think about with great sympathy. In fact, most people consider waiting a waste of time.[1]

—Henri Nouwen

don't wait well. Not for the light to change, not for my line to move in the grocery store (yes, pathologically, I'm one of those people who keeps track of where they would be in other lines), not for my granddaughters to come visit, not for the game to return after a commercial (thank you, DVRs!), not for my turn in the doctor's office. In the words of Inigo Montoya, "I hate waiting."

And I certainly don't like waiting for the time when I get to see Megan again.

Waiting is for my antsy, restless spirit on par with having a cavity filled without the life-is-so-beautiful gas.

You can imagine, then, how I squirm with the realization that Scripture is full of waiting!

I wait for the Lord, my whole being waits,
*   and in his word I put my hope.*
I wait for the Lord
*   more than watchmen wait for the morning,*
*   more than watchmen wait for the morning.*
*   (Ps. 130:5–6)*

In the morning, Lord, you hear my voice;
*   in the morning I lay my requests before you*
*   and wait expectantly. (Ps. 5:3)*

Wait for the Lord;
*   be strong and take heart*
*   and wait for the Lord. (Ps. 27:14)*

We wait in hope for the Lord;
*   he is our help and our shield. (Ps. 33:20)*

Now there was a man in Jerusalem called Simeon,
who was righteous and devout. He was waiting for the
consolation of Israel, and the Holy Spirit was on him.
(Luke 2:25)

But our citizenship is in heaven. And we eagerly await
a Savior from there, the Lord Jesus Christ, who, by the
power that enables him to bring everything under his
control, will transform our lowly bodies so that they will
be like his glorious body. (Phil. 3:20–21)

I get the impression from many Western expressions of Christianity that I'm not the only one who has a hard time waiting. These modern expressions celebrate—rightly so!—what has already happened through the appearing of God's Son, through his death, and through his resurrection. Yet they often fail to realize that this isn't the end. The beginning of the end, perhaps, but not the end itself.

According to Paul, the work of God is two-pronged. First, there was the victory that came through Jesus: sin, the powers of evil, and death were all defeated. But there is more ahead in the future when the final battle is won. Right now, we live in an overlap of the old age and the new age, as indicated in Communion: "For whenever you eat this bread and drink this cup, you proclaim the Lord's death until he comes."

Michael Gorman summarizes Paul's perspective on time well: "The story of God's dream for Israel and for all humanity has come to its climax and is working toward its consummation. . . . This age is passing away, and the new age has begun. To live during the overlap of the ages is to live in a time of great fulfillment and yet also great anticipation."[2]

What triumphalist versions of the Christian story seem to forget is that we're still living in a world that is "passing away"—one that has yet to be fully re-formed by God through the power of Jesus Christ. The reversal of the curse of Genesis 3 has begun, but it isn't complete.

Those who expect all prayers to be answered (the way they want), who promise that all who are poor will become wealthy if they're only faithful, who insist that all who are sick will be cured if they just believe enough—those people are setting others up for great disappointment. Without meaning to, these "summery" Christians can make those of a more wintery disposition feel as if they don't belong—because they struggle with doubt, because they are sick, because they battle ongoing depression, because their marriages aren't hitting on all eight cylinders, or because they can't always face another assembly where it seems as if health, wealth, and happiness are assumed.

Listen: there is a huge NOT YET dimension of the Christian narrative. Even though Jesus has conquered death, it has not been eliminated. Not yet. Even though we have been saved, delivered, and rescued by God, the battle with sin isn't over. Not yet. Even though we know one day God will wipe away all tears from our eyes, the tears aren't gone. Not yet.

GROANING, LONGING, WAITING, HOPING

I want to point to four deep, rich, theologically saturated words from the apostle Paul that we can't live without. These words have a lunar pull on those who are all too familiar with sorrow and grief.

Groaning. "We know that the whole creation has been groaning as in the pains of childbirth right up to the present time" (Rom. 8:22). Groaning is guttural, wordless hope. This Holy Spirit-assisted expression of anticipation recognizes, painfully, that this life has too much illness, hunger, death, sorrow, and grief. Yet it also envisions the grand conclusion of re-creation toward which God is nudging everything along. This groan is the language of our dance between mourning and courageous hope. It recognizes what John Claypool said after his daughter's death: "Courage is worth ten times more than any answer" to the problem of suffering.[3] Groaning recognizes that God is with us, that God hasn't abandoned us, that God hears.

Longing. "Meanwhile we groan, longing to be clothed with our heavenly dwelling, because when we are clothed, we will not be found naked" (2 Cor. 5:2–3). Longing recognizes that this life is full of frailty; it reaches forward into God's future for the fulfillment of his promises regarding "the new heavens and the new earth." It situates us between D-day and V-day (to borrow from Oscar

Cullmann)—knowing the decisive battle is behind but anticipating the final battle (and the shalom) ahead.

Waiting. "The creation waits in eager expectation for the children of God to be revealed" (Rom. 8:19). Waiting is just difficult. Not knowing the ending is torturous. But there's a kind of power in eagerly waiting. We're on tiptoes, straining to observe what God's doing and what God will finally do.

Rather than making us passive and pessimistic, this waiting summons us to courageous living in God's world. I think of Dietrich Bonhoeffer, who was hanged by the Gestapo near the end of the Second World War. He was being punished for taking part in an attempt on Hitler's life. His final words were reported to be: "This is the end, but for me, the beginning!"

As Henri Nouwen observed:

> *There is none of this passivity in Scripture. Those who are waiting are waiting very actively. They know that what they are waiting for is growing from the ground on which they are standing. That's the secret. The secret of waiting is the faith that the seed has been planted, that something has begun. Active waiting means to be present fully to the moment, in the conviction that something is happening where you are and that you want to be present to it. A waiting person is someone who is present to the moment, who believes that this moment is the moment.*[4]

Hoping. "For in this hope we were saved. But hope that is seen is no hope at all. Who hopes for what they already have? But if we hope for what we do not yet have, we wait for it patiently" (Rom. 8:24–25). Paul doesn't use the word like we often do: where it seems like we're hoping against all hope. For him, this hope is built on the firm foundation of the death and resurrection of the Messiah. In a world that is aching from poverty and famine, that is stinging from hurricanes and flooding, that is throbbing from pollution and injustice—in that very world Paul insists that we live with a confident hope in God. It's a hope that renews our strength, that refines our character, that refocuses our desires.

These four words—*groan, long, wait,* and *hope*—attest to us that something is happening, the salvation story is continuing, the redemption is taking place, but it's not here fully, so we should not be surprised when our lives are drenched in seemingly unanswered prayers and tears. Armed with groaning, longing, waiting, and hoping, we don't fall into the pit of despair or try to leap to the peak of final triumph.

How appropriate it is, then, that Paul uses the illustration of pregnancy and childbirth to describe our already/not yet time. I like the way Lee Camp underscores Paul's illustration:

> *Imagine any mother, say, eight months pregnant, on the telephone with an old friend who had heard the news of the pregnancy, but did not know the anticipated date of delivery: "Do you have your baby yet?!" the old friend might ask. To which the mother would undoubtedly be thinking, "—Yes!—of course I've got a baby, of which I'm reminded on every frequent trip to relieve my bladder, or every time the dear one decides to roll over in the womb, or each time she rakes her sweet little arms across my belly." But then again, she does not yet have her baby. To remain eight months pregnant indefinitely would be nothing short of torment. And so she waits for*

the day—and the day comes, with pain and tears. The
mother's body is transformed, and everything changes.
Crying gives way to laughter, cursing gives way to joy, the
groaning gives way to life.[5]

What Paul does affirm is that the God who has loved us and called us in Jesus Christ is still here. Familiar with our tears, God has not abandoned or forsaken us.

In my own life, I've experienced wave upon wave of loss while I've preached and ministered. Those who heard me preach were with me through years of seeing my daughter's health decline, then her death, then "recovering" from the death, then my nephew's death and the "recovering" from that. And then a wreck that almost took my son's life and did take his friend's life. I'm not saying I stand at any epicenter of pain in all these things, but I have had to find a way to live out my faith in the midst of all of this loss. With the help and guidance of friends, I've experienced the oceanic mercy of Christ, the stubbornly steadfast love of the Father, the blanketing presence of the Holy Spirit, even in the midst of the suffering.

The more I feel the groanings, the more I identify with others who also feel them. They are walking with their eyes wide open, observing that there is more pain in the world than one can imagine and seemingly about as much on this side of the cross and resurrection as on the previous side. And many of us wonder: Wasn't the resurrection of Christ supposed to change all this, take away all the decay and sorrow? If Jesus has come and conquered death, if we have been redeemed, if Jesus is King of kings and Lord of lords, then why does it seem at times that nobody's in charge?

Some may think that such questioners, such doubters, are hardly to be called believers. But to be honest, I can't think of anyone who has ever deeply impacted me who did not at times ask these questions. They—and I—cling to these words of Paul: "Who shall separate us from the love of Christ? Shall trouble or hardship or persecution or famine or nakedness or danger or sword? As it is written: 'For your sake we face death all day long; we are considered as sheep to be slaughtered.'"[6]

You could add your own words to the list (trouble, hardship, persecution, famine, nakedness, danger, sword)—those things that make us feel at times like no one is in charge. But here's the startling claim he makes in this magisterial passage: the glory far outweighs the suffering. "No, in all these things we are more than conquerors through him who loved us. For I am convinced that neither death nor life, neither angels nor demons, neither the present nor the future, nor any powers, neither height nor depth, nor anything else in all creation, will be able to separate us from the love of God that is in Christ Jesus our Lord."[7]

And Paul says it's all of creation—the sun, the moon, the stars, the mammals, the birds, the rocks!—they're all on tiptoe, peeking to see what's coming. Paul believes the prophets when they said that God is renewing all of creation. God is restoring—not nuking, not abolishing, not abandoning—all of creation.

So all of creation that is now bound up in thorns and thistles is waiting to see what will happen, wondering, *Will God restore humanity? Is God going to make people into the image of Jesus Christ?*

Creation's beauty is going to be restored and enhanced, so all of creation is waiting for the glorious "not yet."

But even now, in light of the first coming of the Messiah, God is working in all things.[8] "God works together for the good of those who love him" is one of the most quoted snippets of Paul—which is part of the problem, taking snippets of Paul's massive message about what's going on in creation and reducing it to a vapid promise about how "everything works out" for our happiness.

This passage isn't saying that somehow, mysteriously, "all things work together for good" (as in the King James Bible); nor is it indicating that God causes everything that happens. We grieving parents have heard such misguided "wisdom" from well-meaning people far too many times.

Rather, it informs us that God is taking all things—our mistakes, our triumphs, life's joys and fears, all the stuff that's out there—and is producing good.

But a big question remains: What is the "good" Paul is talking about? Does "good" here mean happy lives free of suffering? No. The "good" that God is creating is far more significant: "For those God foreknew he also predestined to be conformed to the image of his Son, that he might be the firstborn among many brothers and sisters. And those he predestined, he also called; those he called, he also justified; those he justified, he also glorified."[9]

The "good" is that God is transforming us into the image of God's Son. That's what this chapter is about. What does it mean to live ethically? What does it mean to be moved along by the Holy Spirit? It means that we are being shaped like Jesus Christ. We become his loving presence in this world. As N. T. Wright insightfully notes, this doesn't take away one bit from our participation with God:

*Is Paul after all a determinist, believing in a blind
plan that determines everything, so that human
freedom, responsibility, obedience, and love itself are
after all a sham? One can easily imagine Paul's own
reaction . . . "Certainly not!" What we have here, rather,
is an expression, as in 1:1, of God's action in setting
people apart for a particular purpose, a purpose in
which their cooperation, their loving response to love,
their obedient response to the personal call, is itself all-
important. This is not to deny the mystery of grace, the
free initiative of God, and the clear divine sovereignty
that is after all the major theme of this entire passage,
here brought to a glorious climax. But it is to deny the
common misconception, based on a two-dimensional
rather than a three-dimensional understanding of how
God's actions and human actions relate to each other,
that sees something done by God as something not done
by humans, and vice versa.[10]*

God is taking everything and laying his trump card on top of it. He's
fashioning something. He's transforming communities into Jesus'
living presence and through them seeking to redeem the whole
world—bringing the life of God, the healing of God to everyone
and everything around them.

Paul's focus, then, isn't on *why* stuff happens—this isn't a
Wikipedia-length solution to the problem of suffering!—but on
what God's doing in all of it. God has big plans for everything.

And so Paul says we are more than conquerors! Try reading
the last half of Romans 8 again from the perspective of Paul, from
the "not yet" perspective of longing and groaning and waiting and

hoping for God to do something in this world about the corruption we see in ourselves, in others, in all of creation.

I consider that our present sufferings are not worth comparing with the glory that will be revealed in us. For the creation waits in eager expectation for the children of God to be revealed. For the creation was subjected to frustration, not by its own choice, but by the will of the one who subjected it, in hope that the creation itself will be liberated from its bondage to decay and brought into the freedom and glory of the children of God.

We know that the whole creation has been groaning as in the pains of childbirth right up to the present time. Not only so, but we ourselves, who have the firstfruits of the Spirit, groan inwardly as we wait eagerly for our adoption, the redemption of our bodies. For in this hope we were saved. But hope that is seen is no hope at all. Who hopes for what they already have? But if we hope for what we do not yet have, we wait for it patiently.

In the same way, the Spirit helps us in our weakness. We do not know what we ought to pray for, but the Spirit himself intercedes for us through wordless groans. And he who searches our hearts knows the mind of the Spirit, because the Spirit intercedes for God's people in accordance with the will of God.

And we know that in all things God works for the good of those who love him, who have been called according to his purpose. For those God foreknew he also predestined to be conformed to the image of his Son, that he might be the firstborn among many brothers and sisters. And those he predestined, he also called; those he called, he also justified; those he justified, he also glorified.

What, then, shall we say in response to these things?
If God is for us, who can be against us? He who did not
spare his own Son, but gave him up for us all—how will
he not also, along with him, graciously give us all things?
Who will bring any charge against those whom God has
chosen? It is God who justifies. Who then can condemn?
No one. Christ Jesus who died—more than that, who
was raised to life—is at the right hand of God and is also
interceding for us. Who shall separate us from the love of
Christ? Shall trouble or hardship or persecution or famine
or nakedness or danger or sword? As it is written:

> *"For your sake we face death all day long;*
> *we are considered as sheep to be slaughtered."*

No, in all these things we are more than conquerors
through him who loved us. For I am convinced that
neither death nor life, neither angels nor demons, neither
the present nor the future, nor any powers, neither height
nor depth, nor anything else in all creation, will be able to
separate us from the love of God that is in Christ Jesus our
Lord. (Rom. 8:18–39)

God took the most heinous act of humanity—the crucifixion of God's own Son—and set it straight, raising him to life. And for those suffering in that hospital, for those of us who walk with a limp, who are clay jars waiting, longing, groaning, and hoping for the redemption of the children of God and all of creation, our faithful God is turning our understanding of the "not-yetness" of life into a new way of walking in spite of the limp: a defiant "AND YET."

15

And Yet

I find that Holy Week is draining; no matter how many times I have lived through his crucifixion, my anxiety about his resurrection is undiminished—I am terrified that, this year, it won't happen; that, that year, it didn't. Anyone can be sentimental about the Nativity; any fool can feel like a Christian at Christmas. But Easter is the main event; if you don't believe in the resurrection, you're not a believer.[1]

—John Irving

I once read Elie Wiesel's *Memoirs*, hoping to learn more about how this man survived the tragedy of the holocaust, losing nearly everyone close to him in the concentration camps.

I think I found what I was looking for when I read that his two favorite words in the English language are the words "AND YET."

Those two words are a powerful rebuttal to the chirpy, syrupy optimism of people who wear rose-colored glasses. They force us to look deep into the dark hole of suffering. Larry Crabb is, in my experience, exactly right about the unrealistic expectations that many Christ-followers (especially in wealthier nations) have today:

Modern Christianity, in dramatic reversal of its biblical form, promises to relieve the pain of living in a fallen world. The message, whether it's from fundamentalists requiring us to live by a favored set of rules or from charismatics urging a deeper surrender to the Spirit's power, is too often the same: The promise of bliss is for now! Complete satisfaction can be ours this side of heaven.

Some speak of the joys of fellowship and obedience, others of a rich awareness of their value and worth. The language may be reassuringly biblical or it may reflect the influence of current psychological thought. Either way, the point of living the Christian life has shifted from knowing and serving Christ till He returns to soothing, or at least learning to ignore, the ache in our soul. . . .

Beneath the surface of everyone's life, especially the more mature, is an ache that will not go away. It can be ignored, disguised, mislabeled, or submerged by a torrent of activity, but it will not disappear. And for good reason. We were designed to enjoy a better world than this. And until that better world comes along, we will groan for what we do not have. An aching soul is evidence not of neurosis or spiritual immaturity, but of realism.

The experience of groaning, however, is precisely what modern Christianity so often tries to help us escape.[2]

These words—AND YET—force us to be honest, but they are also embossed invitations to hope. AND YET invites people blinded by pain and doubt to peek out again with hope-filled vision. They are courageous, defiant words.

For those of us who have lost family and friends in death or have suffered some other kind of painful loss, we're experiencing the downside of love. For, every time we love someone as much as we loved Megan, we become vulnerable. AND YET to have loved her was worth the pain we endured in losing her.

Isn't the old saying right—that it is better to have loved and lost than never to have loved at all? The other option isn't too appealing. As Frederick Buechner has said: "The trouble with steeling yourself against the harshness of reality is that the same steel that secures your life against being destroyed secures your life also against being opened up and transformed by the holy power that life itself comes from."[3]

Those of us who've been crushed can begin to believe that length of life is the most important part of being human. AND YET maybe we're the fools for measuring life more in length than in depth. Some people could be physically alive as long as Methuselah and not live, really live, as much as Megan did in her ten years.

We grieved over how long it will be until we see her again, AND YET from heaven's perspective, the eternal perspective she now shares, the difference between ten years and eighty years must be laughably small.

There's also a lot of sadness because we know the world needed Megan: needed her life, her love, her gentleness. She didn't get to do much. AND YET, Scripture tells us that what is significant in the kingdom is quite different than what we count as significant. For example, when the prophets picture the coming of the kingdom, they envision it as a time when the lion and lamb lie down together. A time when earth's chaos is set aside—freed from hatred and violence.

In such great loss, we become fearful because we sense how difficult the following days, weeks, months, and even years will be. We won't be able to soar with wings like eagles or run and not grow weary, as Isaiah promised. AND YET, in the same passage, God promised that when we couldn't soar or run, we could walk and not faint. I can testify that this promise is true.

Right now, as you are reading this book, you may be experiencing a loss that you've never fully grieved. And this makes me wonder if you've ever fully received the AND YET promises of Jesus.

If you feel like crying, then cry a bucket full of tears.

If you feel like questioning God, then fill a book with your questions.

If some day you think you can't breathe because of grief, let your friends intubate you and breathe for you.

In the process of my daughter's dying, many of us were changed. We were forced to ask questions about life, death, heaven, and angels. We were made to see how foolish all the human energy spent on careers, reputations, and possessions is. We were confronted by her impending death with the preciousness of each day—each moment!

Unbeknownst to us, Megan became our minister. She carried around in her body the suffering and dying of Jesus so that we might see the life of Jesus.

We had to finally say this: Megan is gone, AND YET we will see her again. The hope of seeing my daughter again is a life-giving breath for me.

When my daughter's body was lowered in that plot of ground at Elmwood Cemetery just outside Abilene on Highway 277, it was a cold, rainy day. As I mentioned earlier, I remember hating that it was so wet and cold. She liked being warm and snuggling. I wanted to put some plastic over the fresh dirt to keep the rain off (but didn't).

For the first few months, we drove out there often. Nearly always, Diane and I went separately, lost a bit from each other in our grief. Then as the months rolled into years, our visits were less frequent but still regular.

There are still the three regular dates, of course: Easter (most important), Valentine's Day (when I lay roses), and November 21 (the date of her death). There are other times, like when visitors come to town and want to drive out there. And usually when I'm doing a graveside service at the cemetery, I'll stop by on my way out. But for the most part, the need to visit has diminished through the years.

It is still holy ground, however.

Easter is the most important regular visit. Each year, when a handful of family and friends gathers by Megan's grave at sunrise, these are AND YET gatherings.

Megan's life was so short; AND YET it was full of meaning.

Her frail body was so broken; AND YET she was truly a jar of clay—used by God to hold his precious gospel.

She lived only ten brief years; AND YET, because of the resurrection of Jesus, we believe we will one day see her again.

I can't tell you how many tears I've shed looking forward to that reunion.

Here's my deepest conviction in life: Jesus died a cruel death on the cross one Friday. He was betrayed by one of his followers, denied by one of his best friends, and abandoned by many. He truly is a "man of sorrows, acquainted with grief." AND YET, on Sunday God raised him up so that today he is King of kings and Lord of lords.

❄ ❄ ❄

Through it all, though, Megan's language was singing. She loved to hear music videos. She enjoyed the "ABC Song," "Jesus Loves Me," and "The B-I-B-L-E."

But her favorite song never changed. Megan's greatest desire has now come about. She is now marching in the Lord's army. We have a deep hole of sadness to face because this sweet angel is gone. But we also have buried within us incredible joy because one who could never march in the infantry, ride in the cavalry, or shoot the artillery is now in the Lord's army.

Ten years after Megan's death—ten years down to the minute—I wrote in my journal about our journey of grief and about our joy of anticipation. We were ensconced in the beauty of Sundance in Utah for a wedding I was performing for friends.

It's 10:16 a.m. I've just spoken to everyone at a communion service, centering thoughts on the theme "A River Runs Through It." I wanted to mention Megan and how God's unending stream of mercy has washed and revived us again and again these past ten years. But I didn't. I could tell that if one word came out, I would crack and crumble.

But I remember so well this very minute on 11/21/94. I thought maybe I'd be obsessing more this morning on all those details. But really—since getting up at 4:00 this morning—I've been thinking about what a blessing Megan was.

I can't help but wonder what her last ten years would have been like. I keep thinking about "Searcy Megan"—the energetic little girl who couldn't slow down. But the "Abilene Megan" would have continued to battle sinking health and abilities.

I had a daughter. I'm so blessed. I had a daughter who was beautiful and loving. The years will continue to roll on, but that blessing will never fade. And I'm ten years closer to seeing her than I was!

And yet. Indeed.

16

Always Saturday (for Now)

Ours is the long day's journey of the Saturday. Between
suffering, aloneness, unutterable waste on the one hand
and the dream of liberation, of rebirth on the other.[1]

—George Steiner

My nomination for most heretical typo in a local newspaper goes to the *Abilene Reporter-News*. One year, they asked me to write an editorial piece for Easter. I ended my submission with the words of an old Christian hymn, "One step at a time, dear Savior." But it was printed, "One step at a time, dead Savior." It was an Easter rebuttal!

It makes a difference—a major difference. I remember what a difference it made years ago as I pulled Megan in a red wagon around the quadrangular hallway of a children's hospital. How unfair that encephalitis should strike a child who is already mentally disabled, I kept thinking. As Megan and I kept looping our track, we saw many parents with bleary eyes, many siblings with nervous, awkward laughter, and many kids with IVs and bald heads trying to be brave. Oh, yes, it makes a difference whether the tomb of Jesus was occupied or vacant on Easter morning!

It made a huge difference to Dr. Diane Komp. As a pediatric oncologist, she had a very difficult time believing in a loving God. But in her book *A Window to Heaven,* she recounts how her pilgrimage to faith was guided by her tiny patients and their parents.

She tells of visiting with a mother named Eileen. When this woman's son was diagnosed with leukemia, she enrolled in graduate classes in religious education, hoping for answers. One day, Dr. Komp noticed some books in their hospital room written by theologians who were noted for their skepticism. When asked about them, Eileen explained that she was taking a course titled "Is the Resurrection of Jesus Christ Relevant Today?" So, what did she think? Dr. Komp asked. With great peace and joy, Eileen looked at her son, who was laboring to breathe, and replied, "I know that it's relevant!"[2]

In a later work, Dr. Komp tells of Sammy, a six-year-old with cancer who never responded well to treatment. There were very few days after she met him that he could actually leave the hospital.

Sammy's mom became almost a sister to her. One day, Sammy heard his mother's music: "Our God is an awesome God."

"You're kidding, Mom! God is awesome?"

"Sure he is!"

"God is awesome? Does he wear an earring?"

"Well, he would if he wanted to!"

"Awesome!" was her little one's response.

During his illness, the disease filled Sammy's brain. First it robbed him of his speech, next of his vision, finally of his ability to walk. Never have I felt as frustrated as when that tumor progressed, robbing Sammy of everything that we prize about being human. And yet, Sammy maintained a serenity that was beyond explanation. He could barely move but did what he could without complaint. He could finger his little yellow tape recorder and play his awesome tape.

He was in a room with three other brain-damaged boys, worse off than he, if such was possible. One child had fallen out of a fourth-story window. Another had been beaten. The third was the hapless victim of a hit-and-run driver. The room was a vegetable garden, filled with wilting young life. Mothers sat patiently at their sides, encouraging their sons with their therapy, hoping and praying for a miracle.

The dimples in his steroid-plumped cheeks were flattened out, altering his smile. Sammy used the little strength he had in his right hand to operate his tape recorder. Hannah and I chatted on, discussing his latest test results. From time to time, we would look over to Sammy. He had lain back and listened to his music with the volume turned down so as not to disturb others in the room.

As we spoke, we heard a blast of song: We declare that the kingdom of God is here! The blind see, the deaf hear, the lame man is walking. Sicknesses flee at his voice. The dead live again and the poor hear the good news. Jesus is King, so rejoice! We were startled, as were the others in the room but we all heard the words.

Without being asked, Sammy turned down the volume when that song was finished. He continued to listen quietly to the other songs. Then, with the little strength that he had in the tips of his fingers, he rewound the tape. He played it quietly until he reached the same song. . . .

> *"You really believe that, don't you, kiddo?" I asked. And he nodded vigorously. Sammy believed. But did I? In his childlike faith, this six-year-old found comfort in these words. No, more than comfort. He seemed to find peace and meaning for his life. . . .*
>
> *Sammy and his awesome God shared the secret of his peaceable kingdom.*[3]

The resurrection of Christ is terribly relevant for those who've been victims of injustice. For those who've been gutted by rejection or betrayal. For those who've faced every day with pain—of whatever sort. Or for those who've stood on a wind-kissed hill to pay final respects to a spouse, a child, or a friend.

"I am the resurrection and the life," said Jesus. Either he is or he isn't. It depends on what happened that weekend in Palestine. For those like me who believe that he was raised by his Father, there is wild hope. Suffering and death do not have the final word. A day is coming when pain, failed relationships, bitterness, depression, and death will be put behind us. Jürgen Moltmann had it right: "God weeps with us so that we may someday laugh with him." That's the outrageous joy called Easter!

"It makes a big difference whether we think someone is dead or alive," Luke Timothy Johnson puts it baldly. "The most important question concerning Jesus, then, is simply this: Do we think he is dead or alive?"[4]

What we believe about that question makes all the difference in the world.

KNOWING WHAT TIME IT IS

People need a place where they can set their watches. In my hometown, Pet Milk was the ultimate authority. People in Neosho, Missouri, could set their watches by the noon whistle. It was an authority that wasn't to be questioned—although there always lingered the uncertainty of where the whistle-blower at Pet Milk set his watch!

So much of Christian living is figuring out and remembering what time it is. Week after week, we help one another recalibrate our time frames.

I like the tradition of a Baptist church in Abilene. Every spring when it's time to set clocks forward an hour—so that non-church-attenders don't notice it while church-attenders are punished (since they have to finish their sleep in hard pews)—this church waits until they meet the next morning. They get their full night's sleep. Then together they roll their watches forward from 10:00 to 11:00. I love this picture: a church gathered on Sunday to make sure everyone knows what time it is.

As we've seen, our two central reference points are the ones Communion spotlights each week: "For whenever you eat this bread and drink this cup, you proclaim the Lord's death until he comes."[5] Our first reference point is the death and resurrection of Jesus; the second is the future return of Jesus. The first is the pivotal event of all history. The second is the inevitable culmination of that event.

Paul was quite familiar with the apocalyptic time frame: this evil age and the age of God to come. But while his language is similar, it also has a unique twist. To Paul, the end has already begun. In other words, there is an overlap of the two ages, and it's in this overlap that God's people live.

The old age is one marked by sin. It is the world of death, of pride, of lust, of disregard for God. It is the place of despair and hopelessness. It's a time when old prejudices are savored, and hurt feelings are cherished.

The new age is the one marked by grace and by freedom from sin. It is where life is oriented around God and his rule. It is the realm where humans are freed from the evil forces that previously kept a gun to their heads with bullets like fear, anxiety, and meaninglessness.

God's people are already a part of this new age. We already have eternal life; we already have forgiveness; we have already been delivered from our sins and passions. But we have not yet fully experienced the new age. For while we have been saved from sins, we still sin. While we have already been forgiven, we still need forgiveness. While we have been raised to walk in new life, we still face death.

It is the job of believers to keep reminding one another what time it is. We, like Communion, proclaim the Lord's death until he comes.

We announce the good news that we aren't stuck in Friday—when there is nothing but darkness covering the earth, when doom and gloom prevail. A funeral dirge shouldn't be our theme song!

But we also announce that it isn't quite Sunday—when darkness is completely past, when we fully experience the resurrection, when all tears are wiped away from our eyes. And so the New Song of Revelation doesn't quite fit as a theme song either.

We live in Saturday—between the old age of Friday and the new age of Sunday. In our congregations are those who live in the despair of Friday and others who've leaped over Saturday into the fullness of Sunday. To both groups, we announce week after week that it is Saturday. We have already but not yet fully been saved. We have already but not yet fully received eternal life.

Every aspect of Christian living must be kept in this framework of a kingdom that has been inaugurated but not consummated. If our time frame is skewed, our lives will be as well. We prod the stubborn of faith to believe what God has already done through Christ. And we warn the naive of faith that the final victory remains. In other words, we continue proclaiming the Lord's death until he comes.

And this hope, "until he comes," is what we continue to cling to when we remember Megan. Since the spring of 1995, our little band of family and friends has gathered at a West Texas cemetery early on Easter morning. Our ritual is always brief and simple. We share a few Megan stories, remember how she enriched our lives, read 1 Corinthians 15, and pray. Then we join our church family to remember that Jesus is our living Lord who is present among us through the Spirit and who is coming again.

I wish there were some way to shield people I love from grief and loss. But there just isn't. As Joy Gresham says to C. S. Lewis in *Shadowlands*, "The pain now is part of the happiness then. That's the deal."

And the death of a child, while traumatic, certainly isn't the only kind of loss people in the community of faith suffer. We experience the loss of youth, the loss of love, the loss of dreams, the loss of health, and the loss of relationships. We grieve for mothers who have miscarried and for marriages that have failed; for people who have lost their jobs; and for teens who have lost their bearings.

But thanks to the resurrection of Jesus, we can search for meaning in the midst of our losses. We relearn how to be in the world. We reinterpret our personal stories, taking into account the losses we've suffered. Ironically, these very losses often make life (and what matters in life!) much clearer. David Wolpe writes:

> *My deepest prayer to God used to be to spare me from the pains of life that I so dreaded. Now I see that that is the prayer of a child. As a man I do not pray for a life without pain. Instead I pray: "Dear God, I know that there will be pain in my life, and sadness, and loss. Please give me the strength to create a life, together with those whom I love, where loss will not be empty, where pain will not be purposeless. Help me find the faith to make loss matter. Amen."[6]*

In our losses, we cry, lament, groan, question, and wait. But there's one thing we won't do: despair. For we live in hope. We are the people of Easter: those who have already believed in and experienced the Resurrected One. We long for his power to be completely manifest and for every tear to be wiped away. So we pray, "*Marana Tha* . . . Come, O Lord."

17

Whistling Again

*What I have learned is something stranger still: Suffering
may be among the sufferer's blessings. I think of a former
colleague who, upon recovering from a heart attack,
remarked that he would not have missed it for the life of
him. In the valley of suffering, despair and bitterness are
brewed. But there also character is made. The valley of
suffering is the vale of soul-making.[1]*

—Nicholas Wolterstorff

*You turned my wailing into dancing;
you removed my sackcloth and clothed me with joy.*

—Psalm 30:11

Here's a little-known fact that many who have lost a child can
testify to: life starts to make sense again shortly after the
funeral . . . just before it falls apart and makes no sense at all. You
realize that your life is going to continue, but your child will not
be there. Ever.

Four and a half years after Megan's death, my brother and my
sister-in-law received the tragic news that their baseball-playing,

fish-catching, joke-telling son, Jantsen, had died suddenly at the age of fifteen. We dropped everything and drove back to Missouri.

It was the longest nine hours I've ever spent in a car. Oklahoma seemed never-ending as we inched our way from Texas to Missouri. My nephew—the life of a party with a heart of pure compassion— had gone to lift weights with his football team and was resting afterward when his heart quit working. He'd had an undetected heart defect and no prior indications that he was at risk. Randy and Pam received a call that something was wrong, hurried to the house to find paramedics trying to revive him, followed the ambulance to the hospital, and then paced the floor with family and friends just as the doctor said, "I'm sorry. He's gone."

Mile after mile I drove, wishing I'd rented a plane to take us. I knew too much about the large, looming grief they faced. I knew they didn't yet know that every day would feel worse than the previous day for quite a while . . . that loving friends would get back to their lives while their own lives would seem to stop . . . and that faith would help but not be a magic salve.

When we finally got to their house, one of Pam's relatives said, "He's back in the bedroom waiting for you." As I walked in, Randy gave a huge, first-recognition smile, then one second later collapsed into sobs.

We had shared a room as kids; we'd ridden ponies and bikes and played endless games of football and basketball; I'd performed his wedding ceremony.

And now we were two grieving fathers in each other's arms.

He choked out the words, "I'm so sorry."

"What do you mean?" I asked.

"I'm just so sorry about Megan. If I'd known how painful it is, I would have called more often."

I assured him that no one can know. It's a private club of grief. No member hopes for more members. We don't recruit.

Randy, Pam, and Crista, their daughter, made it through the funeral. Kind, comforting words were spoken as we remembered Jantsen's short, powerful life, and as we attempted to comfort each other. The following week, Randy and I took walks each morning. He was numb—and yet he was walking and talking. Processing grief starts with little things like eating when you don't want to eat and speaking to someone when you'd rather hide in a cave.

For most parents who lose children, this is when the bottom drops out.

But something amazing happened. No, they were not relieved of their grief. They—like my family—will live with a measure of grief the rest of their lives. But something happened that would, over the course of the next decade, make the words of the psalmist, "You turned my mourning into dancing," become a reality in our lives that we never imagined we'd see and experience firsthand.

This is the story of a mother's and father's love even after the death of their son. A story so woven with my own that it's hard to tell, but it's too filled with surprising redemption to suppress anymore.

When Jantsen died, Pam and Randy made a decision that many families make these days: to set up a memorial fund in Jantsen's name in lieu of flowers at the funeral. But that simple decision led to another and another, and eventually it led to a decision that no other family I know has ever made—one that inspired Oprah Winfrey to give Pam a standing ovation.

To their surprise, the fund accumulated an amazing twenty-five thousand dollars. They thought of buying uniforms for Neosho sports teams or playground equipment for the parks, but other funds were available for those. A *New York Times* piece narrates what happened next:

> *"It got to the point it was almost comical," Mrs. Cope said. "All the doors were closed. That's when we decided that God had very specific plans for this money and that our money should be spent overseas."*
>
> *They finally offered the money to Arkansas friends who were building orphanages in Vietnam.*[2]

Before Jantsen's death, normal life for my brother's family was a lot like that of many other Americans, with life revolving around baseball games, my niece's dance lessons, and careers. Pam had owned a hair salon in Neosho, the tiny southwest Missouri town where I grew up. Randy had just been promoted to vice president of a newspaper company that ran papers all over the country. Even to a *New York Times* reporter, Pam admitted, "My world was very small. I was pretty shallow."

But all that changed the day Jantsen died. Pam said she knew that with his death, they could never simply resume normal life again. They would be transformed by Jantsen's death and the events and decisions to come. But they had to come through deep grief to find a new focus.

My brother wrote about those days and months following Jantsen's death and how he struggled to find a new normal.

Actually, I knew that it had changed the moment the doctor came out of the emergency room and told my wife and me that our fifteen-year-old son had passed from this life from what we later found out was an undetected heart problem.

I had enjoyed my life up to that point—a healthy family, a good job, and a bright future—but as I stood in the hallway of Freeman Hospital, there was no doubt that things would never be the same. Before I left my son's side that day, I prepared myself for a life that resembled a scorched forest after a wild fire. The hillsides filled with lush trees and the valleys filled with wildflowers would now be smoldering ashes.

As the fog lifted, so did the reality of what had been lost. Each new act brought new pain—the first trip to the store, the first Sunday at church—even the first time I decided to make oatmeal and had to figure out how to make it for one person, since he and I were the only breakfast eaters in the house.

And such was my life—for a season.

Yet one day, months later, I caught myself whistling.

There wasn't much life in the tune, but it surprised me just the same. As I look back on it now, I see that moment as a sign of the renewal that was to follow.

It was about the time that Randy learned to whistle again that they decided to go to Vietnam to see how the twenty-five thousand dollars was being used. What they saw there shocked them.

They saw children on the streets fending for their lives. They saw poverty like nothing they'd experienced or seen up close before. As they walked the streets in cities like Saigon and Danang, children approached them, begging for money and food. They soon learned that these children are commonly known as "doi moi," *dust of the earth.* They were not only starving for food but for every other thing children need, such as education and love. They were at risk of being picked up and abused by child traffickers and forced to work in hard labor or sexual bondage.

What they saw further broke their already grieving hearts.

Hoping to do their part to save at least a few children from this fate—and a tortured future in slavery—Pam and Randy decided to partner with volunteers in Vietnam and use Jantsen's gift to rent a house in Saigon, hire houseparents, and bring in fifteen children who would be given a permanent home, an education, medical care, and a chance to be part of a family.

A few months later, they rented another house, brought home fifteen more kids, and the Touch A Life Foundation was born.

But they didn't stop at working only in Vietnam. In Cambodia, they helped finance a shelter for families suffering from AIDS-related illnesses. Neither did they leave those problems far away: they adopted two orphaned Vietnamese children.

Randy said Pam was in so much pain after Jantsen's death, but he watched her fight through her grief and turn her love to other kids. This inspired my brother to join her and help start and run the Touch A Life Foundation.

But during those dark days of grief, even as they helped other children, he felt like giving up. He wrote this note to family members a few months after Jantsen's death.

I can really relate to the folks that lost sons and daughters while making their way across the country on the Oregon Trail. An estimated fifty thousand people lost their lives

on this two thousand mile journey—many of whom, I'm
sure, were children.

Losing a child is hard enough, but the thought of
loading the wagons back up and moving on must have
been devastating. I'm sure the parents wanted to just tell
the rest of them to go on, that they would stay there where
their child had died.

I'm sure there were parents, like Pam and I, who lost
children, like Jantsen, and felt like just building a small
cabin near the grave and living out their life in solitude.
That is how I would have felt.

In fact, that is how I feel right now.

I don't want to keep moving down the trail. I just
want to tell everyone to go on without me. Jantsen meant
too much to me to just put a headstone on his grave and
go on without him. I can't go on with my career or start
new projects or dream new dreams.

I can't go on.

So why did they? Why did the parents that lost their
precious children move on? Maybe it was because their
decision was so black and white. Either they stayed out on
the plains of Kansas and tried to survive by themselves or
they moved on.

In a matter of days, they were forced to decide
not what they wanted to do, but what was best for
their family.

What would God have them do? Live out their life in
seclusion or go on and be an inspiration to others?

What would their child have them do? Spend their
life fighting the elements on their own or go with the others
to the beautiful valleys of Oregon?

Looking back, it would seem an easy decision. After
all, their child is with the Lord in heaven, and there were
so many promising things on down the trail.

But it wasn't that easy. In fact, I'm sure there were those that stayed behind.

I can't say for sure that I can move on at this point. I don't have the energy, I don't have the drive, and I don't have the longing to move on.

Yet in some ways, I already am. I feel like I am standing not on a trail, but in a powerful river—a river that pushes me away from my past—away from Jantsen. I'm fighting the current trying to stay with my son, but I just seem to be getting further and further away.

I am not ready to make a decision to leave him; yet I am moving further from him every day.

Is this current the "time" that everyone tells me will make things better? If so, why do I feel I am fighting it rather than it helping me?

Yet, whether a trail or a winding river, I realize God's will is for me to move on. I sense that the work he has for me is work that can't be done from beside Jantsen's grave.

But I am not ready to leave yet.

For now, I will stay kneeled beside the trail at this sacred place that future generations won't remember, but that I'll never forget.

Their visit to Vietnam opened a startling new world of human needs to Randy and Pam. They began to see the urgency of the prayer that Jesus taught:

Thy kingdom come,
Thy will be done on earth as it is in heaven.

Jesus had announced in his hometown synagogue that God's Spirit anointed him to proclaim good news to the poor, to proclaim freedom for the prisoners and recovery of sight for the blind, to set the oppressed free, and to proclaim the year of the Lord's favor (Luke 4:16–30).

Randy and Pam realized as they felt wave upon wave of human need that the way of Jesus—even in their brokenness and grief—was sending them into a world in deep need of God's shalom.

There, on Thanksgiving Day, 1999, they met a boy in one of the orphanages whom they decided they couldn't leave. That's now my nephew, Van. Later, they would also adopt a girl, Tatum. As my brother put it:

> *In a country around the world,*
> *In a land rich with history,*
> *In a province full of beauty,*
> *In a town bustling with activity,*
> *In a center filled with hope,*
> *In a room built with love,*
> *Against a wall supported by dreams,*
> *We found our new child,*
> *A precious soul,*
> *His name—Van Alan Cope.*

In 2006, Touch A Life (TAL) expanded their work across the globe to Ghana, West Africa, after Pam and Randy read an article in *The New York Times* about the thriving child slave trade there. Thousands of children, some as young as five years old, are sold to work in the fishing industry or as domestic servants in the Lake Volta region.

After learning of the neglect and abuse these children are forced to endure on a daily basis, they knew that TAL had to get involved. To date, working in partnership with a remarkable team of Ghanaians, TAL has rescued sixty-eight children from slavery and built a residential facility where these former slave children can live, receive an education, and have a chance at hope.

In April of 2009, Pam's memoir *Jantsen's Gift: A True Story of Grief, Rescue, and Grace* was published to critical acclaim, including a standing ovation led by Oprah.

Pam has become a champion for children's rights around the world. *The New York Times* article continues:

> *Initially, she found fund-raising stressful. "I would speak to 400 or 500 people, and nobody would give me any money," she said. Then, she said, she decided she could only try to be a voice for children in crisis, not control the reaction. Now she views the balance sheet with equanimity.*
>
> *"Money comes from places I never expect, and places I expect to get money from I don't," she said. "Part of my message is, you don't have to have tons of money, but you have to have a willing heart."*
>
> *Hers was touched Oct. 29 by the plight of Ghanaian children who were forced to labor up to 14 hours a day for fishermen on Lake Volta. The Copes read an article in The New York Times that day about how the child workers in fishing villages around Kete Krachi were deprived of necessities, schooling and freedom.*
>
> *The International Organization for Migration, an intergovernmental group that fights child trafficking, was planning a long-term rescue project there. Late in January, working with officials from the Ministry of Women and Children in Ghana, it secured the freedom of 25 children, its first group from Kete Krachi.*

But Mrs. Cope did not want to wait to see if the International Organization for Migration would come through. Working from her home in November, she teamed up with a Kete Krachi schoolteacher, George Achibra, and a Dutch volunteer, Paul van den Bosch. The men run Pacodep, a small nonprofit group in Ghana. It also aids International Organization for Migration programs.

Mr. Achibra and Mr. van den Bosch negotiated with the employers of seven children, offering to pay for new nets, boat repairs and other needs in exchange for the children's freedom. The two tracked down the parents of those children. All of the destitute parents agreed in writing that their children should be cared for at a Christian-run orphanage called The Village of Hope, Mr. van den Bosch said.

Four days before Christmas, the children arrived by bus at the orphanage. Caregivers said one girl was so fearful of going hungry that she filled a bag with leftovers from other children's plates. Few of the children had had any schooling. All now attend school.

When Mrs. Cope visited in January, she found Mark Kwadwo a transformed child—reveling in piggyback rides, spaghetti and his new school uniform.

"To hear him giggle," she wrote by e-mail, "was priceless."

In the summer of 2009, Pam wrote this letter to Mark Kwadwo to let him know what a part of their lives he had become.

Dear Mark,

If there's one thing I've learned in my life, it's that time goes too quickly. Before we know it, in a blink of an eye, or an irregular heart beat, everything we have can be gone.

Without warning. Without a chance to even say good-bye. So I'm writing you this letter, just as I sometimes do for my other children, so you always know exactly where you stand.

I will never forget how I first met you, in a color photograph in The New York Times. *Seeing how you looked then—your dirty t-shirt and your scarred skin and that fear in your eyes—I was so saddened for you, and filled with a desire to help you. I thought at the time that that just wasn't possible. You seemed so far away. You seemed so foreign. I couldn't even locate the country where you lived on a map.*

It's strange now to think about that. You've become such an important part of our family. It's almost like I can't remember a time when your artwork wasn't hanging on our wall, the first thing I see when I walk out the door to take the kids to school; or when that photo of you—smiling and goofy—wasn't on the fridge. I think I keep these reminders of you not only so I can remember to write you a letter, or give you a call, but to remind myself of everything you've taught me, and the person you've helped me to become.

People say I rescued you. But Mark, I want you to know something. You've also rescued me. You have taught me so many things. About love, and grace, and courage. About what it means to be and to have a family. You have changed my very idea of motherhood. Being a mother doesn't just mean that I parent the children I've given birth to, or the ones I've adopted. I now understand that being a mother means that we make ourselves available to children, regardless of where they live, or the language that they speak. I take great pride in being scolded by the staff at Village of Hope because I brought you too much candy. That is just what moms do for their kids.

*The first time I came to visit you, I remember
watching you cook your pot of beans on an open fire
with your roommates—the boys you now call brothers.
To see you poking the fire with a stick, and the way you
embraced life as a normal six-year-old, you taught me
that beauty truly does come from ashes. Everything and
every life can be restored. You and I will always have the
scars to remind us from where we came and what we've
endured. As we both know, dark backgrounds help the
diamonds shine even brighter.*

*When I look around at all of the people I have met
who want to do whatever they can to help you, and the
thousands of other children who have been sold into
slavery, I've learned that I am a part of a big, caring, and
generous community. A community of people who are
willing to look and live outside of themselves.*

*Watching you get excited about your bowl of rice in
the morning, and a clean glass of water, you've taught me
that life is the loveliest when it's the most simple.*

*You've taught me how crazy I am to try and
complicate it so much; and to fill it with things that don't
matter. With things that won't last. Money. Possessions.
Frantic schedules. Self-absorption.*

*You've taught me the value in making connections;
and the indescribable importance of a true friend. As I
look around the room now, at these amazing, funny, wild,
and courageous women, I remember you.*

*And most of all, you have taught me the one thing I
never thought I'd learn. Every single one of us, regardless
of how bad it is, can overcome our very worst situation.
Abuse, the loss of a mother, a friend, or a beautiful
fifteen-year-old son who, when he left my world, I was
sure that I'd never truly live again. You have helped me to
live again.*

And you make me want to keep working, to work myself right out of this job. You make me want to tell your story so often and so many times, that people know it by heart. I want them to want to help you, or someone like you. Hopefully it would be one of the seven thousand kids who are still enslaved, but maybe not. Maybe it's someone else. Someone in their own community, in their own house. Maybe it's just a decision they make to finally take care of themselves.

I have so many more things to say to you but for now I want to say this. Thank you. In finding you, I have found myself. I have found my Mark. And now I will do what I can, to help others do the same. My beautiful, awesome friends, I have found my Mark. Are you ready to find yours?

Love,
Mama Pam

This is by no means the life that my brother and sister-in-law had in mind. It's so much sadder. And yet so much more meaningful.

Would they receive Jantsen back if they could? Absolutely! And yet, in their loss, God led them far beyond their own lives into the world he loves . . . to the poor, to orphans, to grieving parents, and to—yes—child slaves.

In some ways, it began when my brother caught himself whistling—a sign of grace that life wasn't over.

He and I have suffered the losses of our children—of Megan and of Jantsen—but their joy and their love live on as we await God's ultimate burst of shalom.

18

Nostos

To be homeless the way people like you and me are apt to be homeless is to have homes all over the place but not to be really at home in any of them.[1]

—Frederick Buechner

By necessity, I made my own private treaty with rootlessness and spent my whole life trying to fake or invent a sense of place. Home is a foreign word in my vocabulary and always will be.[2]

—Pat Conroy

t was May 11, 1857, when Joel and Susan Trotter, my great-great-great grandparents, left their home in Missouri. Inspired by the gold rush and the dream of sudden wealth, they packed their possessions, loaded their wagons, gathered their herd of cattle, and headed west to California. They followed the Oregon Trail, much of which had been blazed by Susan's first cousin, Meriwether Lewis.

In many ways, this journey is still alive in our family today, thanks to a journal that my great-great-great grandmother kept. On the day she left, she wrote:

We have this day bid adieu to our homes and friends, and commenced our journey toward California. It is a trying thing to part with our beloved friends, perhaps to see them no more on earth, and partly when we are beginning a journey that is attributed with so much danger and fatigue as the one we have undertaken.

The journal is filled with thrilling stories and mundane details ("plenty of grass for cattle" . . . "adequate grass") along the way.

The Trotters eventually made it to California, the land of fortune and opportunity.

But she never quit missing home—so much so that eventually they repacked their belongings and headed back to Missouri.

They went home.

The strong pull of home was expressed by the Greeks in a word: *nostos*. It means "homecoming." One of the poems in the Epic Cycle is entitled *Nostoi* (the plural form)—a celebration of the return of the Greek heroes to their homes following the Trojan War.

Of course, the most celebrated *nostos* was that of Odysseus. After being gone from his home in Ithaca and from his wife, Penelope, for two decades, he battled the offended gods, the uncooperative winds, the sea monsters, and his opponents on land in order to get back to his beloved home.

Along the way, he and his men met up with the lotus-eaters—people who tried to get them to eat the lotus fruit, which would make them forget about home. So Homer has Odysseus report:

All [the men] now wished for was to stay where they were with the lotus-eaters, to browse on the lotus, and to forget that they had a home to return to. I had to use force to

bring them back to the ships, and they wept on the way,
but once on board I dragged them under the benches and
left them in irons. I then commanded the rest of my loyal
band to embark with all speed on their fast ships, for fear
that others of them might eat of the lotus and think no
more of home.

What a tragedy that would be: to think no more of home. For something deep inside of us is longing for home.

Think of David, trapped behind enemy lines, longing for a drink from a well in his hometown of Bethlehem. That's a pretty strong sense of nostalgia (a word that comes from *nostos*—literally, an aching for home).

Imagine the Israelites in exile longing for Jerusalem, Dorothy wanting to return to Kansas, or Sam and Frodo missing the Shire.

Isn't this much of the success behind Marilynne Robinson's *Gilead*, Garrison Keillor's Lake Wobegon, or Philip Gulley's *Harmony*? These are places we'd love to go back to.

A part of me still misses Neosho, the small town in southwestern Missouri where I was born, where I was raised, and where I graduated from high school. It is Lake Wobegon—a place of unique characters, courageous lives, and children who are all above average. It's where I memorized much of the book of Acts as a boy; where I played Little League ball; where my dad first let go of the back of my Schwinn bike; where I hung out with my maternal granddad and my dad at the newspaper office; where I stayed up "late" (9:00 P.M.) with my maternal grandmother and my cool young aunt playing Monopoly and Clue; where my paternal grandparents drilled me on books of the Bible and state capitals (Nevada?

Carson City); where I shared a room with my brother. And where I left in the fall of 1974.

Of course, Thomas Wolfe was right: in a sense you can't ever go home again. For the home you knew has changed. Or it turns out to be more complicated than you remember it.

In one of Frederick Buechner's novels, a young man named Antonio Parr returns to his home. He's welcomed by a sign some children have made that says: WELCOME HONE. The slight misspelling on the sign turned out to be symbolic, for no homecoming in this life is perfect! Parr says: "It seemed oddly fitting. It was good to get home, but it was home with something missing or out of whack about it. It wasn't much, to be sure, just some minor stroke or serif, but even a minor stroke can make a major difference."[3]

Since Megan's death, I've had an urgent sense of *nostos*, of homecoming, of reunion. I dreamed for years about a time when I would hold her again. I miss(ed) her big, eager eyes and the way she slung a leg over me while I fed her and the fresh smell of her hair and the little noises that she and only she could make (and found joy in making, knowing they were unique to her).

For a couple of years after Megan's death, Diane wrote letters to Megan in her journal. It's clear that she, too, has this burning longing for *nostos*. In her letter on the first anniversary of Megan's death, she wrote:

Dear Megan,

I have missed you terribly today! I have now crossed into a new realm in time: I no longer can say that last year at this time you were with me. Last year at this time my arms were empty. This brings great sadness in me. Time moves too swiftly and yet too slowly!

I spent the entire day weeping. Yet in the midst of the dark hole, God did bring me a blessing. The blessing came at your grave. After crying for a while, I decided to read the Psalms aloud. I began reading the praise psalms. An inner thought I believe to be the Holy Spirit told me to go to the book of Isaiah. I don't know that book very well, so I began reading subtitles to see where to stop and read. I came to chapter 25 because the subtitle was "Praise to the Lord." This seemed to stay with my theme, so I began reading.

It was truly amazing! I knew that the Lord was speaking to me. That he was present in my pain for you—even at your grave. Verse 8 was where the bells would have chimed if I had any. It's where the thunder rang out—where the applause came.

He will swallow up death forever.

The Sovereign Lord will wipe away the tears from all faces!

I knew that was the verse God wanted me to see. I must admit a part of me became angry because I don't believe it will be in my lifetime. Some other mother or father will reap the benefit of having their child back immediately. But at that moment, another insight hit me: that death will not prevail. God is the ultimate winner! Satan loves death and all it brings. God despises it and aches for and with us.

But God will prevail, and there will be a time when there will no longer be death and no longer be tears.

Praise God!!! I can't wait!!!

Love,
Mom

This is the kind of anticipation that fills the pages of Scripture. It's the hopeful vision in the last part of Isaiah:

"See, I will create
*   new heavens and a new earth.*
The former things will not be remembered,
*   nor will they come to mind.*
But be glad and rejoice forever
*   in what I will create,*
for I will create Jerusalem to be a delight
*   and its people a joy.*
I will rejoice over Jerusalem
*   and take delight in my people;*
the sound of weeping and of crying
*   will be heard in it no more.*

"Never again will there be in it
*   infants who live but a few days,*
*   or older people who do not live out their years;*
those who die at a hundred
*   will be thought mere youths;*
those who fail to reach a hundred
*   will be considered accursed.*
They will build houses and dwell in them;
*   they will plant vineyards and eat their fruit.*
No longer will they build houses and others live in them,
*   or plant and others eat.*
For as the days of a tree,
*   so will be the days of my people;*
my chosen ones will long enjoy
*   the work of their hands.*
They will not labor in vain,
*   nor will they bear children doomed to misfortune;*
for they will be a people blessed by the Lord,

they and their descendants with them.
Before they call I will answer;
    while they are still speaking I will hear.
The wolf and the lamb will feed together,
    and the lion will eat straw like the ox,
    but dust will be the serpent's food.
They will neither harm nor destroy
    on all my holy mountain,"
    says the Lord. (Isa. 65:17–25)

As N. T. Wright summarizes: "To put it bluntly, creation is to be redeemed; that is, space is to be redeemed, time is to be redeemed, and matter is to be redeemed."[4]

It's also the forward-looking message of Hebrews 11, when the author says: "All these people were still living by faith when they died. They did not receive the things promised; they only saw them and welcomed them from a distance, admitting that they were foreigners and strangers on earth. People who say such things show that they are looking for a country of their own."[5]

Hebrews imagines us on a journey to a time of reunion, of rest, of ultimate fellowship. It anticipates the renewal of all things by God.

In the powerful words of Wendell Berry:

And this, then,
is the vision of that Heaven of which
we have heard, where those who love
each other have forgiven each other,
where, for that, the leaves are green,
the light a music in the air,
and all is unentangled,
and all is undismayed.[6]

"All is unentangled." What a great way to describe God's promised future. In fact, that could be a *Reader's Digest* version of the New Jerusalem in the final chapters of Revelation: "All is unentangled." It is home in the deepest sense because God is present—as hinted at by Frederick Buechner:

> *I cannot claim that I have found the home I long for every day of my life, not by a long shot, but I believe that in my heart I have found, and have maybe always known, the way that leads to it. I believe that . . . the home we long for and belong to is finally where Christ is. I believe that home is Christ's kingdom, which exists both within us and among us as we wend our prodigal ways through the world in search of it.*[7]

I'm thinking now back to some of the final words of my friend Don Bowen. A nationally known and distinguished plaintiffs' attorney, Don was also a valued and loved member of our church who shared his grief and his hope with our church family.

He was considered one of the best lawyers in Texas, and he fought for the rights of people in thousands of cases in his career. His work representing Exxon after the Valdez oil spill against its insurers secured massive amounts of funding for cleanup—the prominence of which may obscure somewhat the fact that he fought for the rights of the everyday citizen.

I was in the hospital room with him when his longtime family doctor came in to tell him he had pancreatic cancer. In the months following that diagnosis, many promised him that God would heal him.

Don just pressed forward with quiet faith.

Three months before his death at age fifty-six, I asked him to share Communion thoughts with our church. Here are his words that remain among the most powerful I've ever heard spoken:

There are some things that I don't know, but there are some things I do know.

God is in control.

I believe that with all my heart. I know that God can do any miracle he desires. I know that if it is God's plan, he can heal me. But I want you to understand that I also know this: my physical well being is not a test for God; it is not a test of God's mercy; it is not a test for the faithfulness of this church; it is not a test for the power of your prayers; because God has healed me.

He has healed every one of us that has already called on his name. I know that just as well as I know my own name. I know that I have been healed, and I have been forgiven. God has forgiven me, and he has saved me.

We know how all this comes out.

This is the beauty of all of this. We have no confusion about how all this comes out. We see a lot of the power of Satan in the world, but we know that the battle has been won by God. It is not a negotiated peace; it is over. God won. Whatever God's plan is for my physical health, I pray that my family's faith will remain strong and that this church's faith will remain strong.

May the Spirit of Christ be renewed in each of us. May the saltiness of our tears wash away our doubts and all our fears. May we claim quiet strength in suffering. May we never, never lose our faith in God. May each heart here be filled to overflowing with God's hope. May our united voices proclaim God's healing love for each of our souls, no matter what happens. May we say to each other and the world around us, "God will take care of us."

All this sense of longing I have for home in this life is a hint of the greater longing in my heart. It's a longing for the time of God's new creation; a time for the restoration of all things; a time when God is all in all; a time when God's kingdom has come and his will has been done on earth as it is in heaven.

THE NEXT KISS

When Megan was just five, she was playing in our fenced-in backyard. I was supposed to be keeping a close eye on her, but of course Diane and I defined "close" very differently.

I looked out after a few minutes to see Megan's face down by the dog's food dish. She was picking up the dog food and eating it. I ran outside and said, "Megan!"

She knew she was toast. Limited comprehension or not, she knew that eating the dog's food was a no-no. I walked toward her, having no idea yet what to do. Just as I reached her, she puckered her lips for a kiss.

What a picture: a little girl with her glasses on, crumbs on her face, and dog breath, puckered up for a kiss.

I'm so glad I didn't let that invitation pass. It was a kiss only a parent could enjoy.

I now await that next kiss. I eagerly await God's final work of new creation. A time to set things right. A time to wipe away all tears.

And a time to be reunited with Megan, my daughter and my teacher.

On the Death of the Beloved

by John O'Donohue

Though we need to weep your loss,
You dwell in that safe place in our hearts
Where no storm or night or pain can reach you.

Your love was like the dawn
Brightening over our lives,
Awakening beneath the dark
A further adventure of colour.

The sound of your voice
Found for us
A new music
That brightened everything.

Whatever you enfolded in your gaze
Quickened in the joy of its being;
You placed smiles like flowers
On the altar of the heart.
Your mind always sparkled
With wonder at things.

Though your days here were brief,
Your spirit was alive, awake, complete.

We look toward each other no longer
From the old distance of our names;
Now you dwell inside the rhythm of breath,
As close to us as we are to ourselves.

Though we cannot see you with outward eyes,
We know our soul's gaze is upon your face,

Smiling back at us from within everything
To which we bring our best refinement.

Let us not look for you only in memory,
Where we would grow lonely without you.
You would want us to find you in presence,
Beside us when beauty brightens,
When kindness glows
And music echoes eternal tones.

When orchids brighten the earth,
Darkest winter has turned to spring;
May this dark grief flower with hope
In every heart that loves you.

May you continue to inspire us:
To enter each day with a generous heart.
To serve the call of courage and love
Until we see your beautiful face again
In that land where there is no more separation,
Where all tears will be wiped from our mind,
And where we will never lose you again.[8]

Notes

Introduction

1. Henri Nouwen, *Adam* (Maryknoll, N.Y.: Orbis Books, 1997), 56, 127.

First Secret: God Is a Heart Specialist

Chapter One

1. Morris West, *The Clowns of God* (New Milford, Conn.: Toby Press, 2003).
2. Jessica Cohen, "Grade A: The Market for a Yale Woman's Eggs," *Atlantic Monthly*, December 2002.

Chapter Two

1. Eugene Peterson, *The Jesus Way* (Grand Rapids, Mich.: Eerdmans, 2007), 79.
2. Joan Jacobs Brumberg, *The Body Project* (New York: Random House, 1997), xxiv.
3. 1 Samuel 16:7.
4. Anne Lamott, *Traveling Mercies* (New York: Random House, 1999), 203–205.
5. Luke 16:15.
6. Barbara Brown Taylor, *Bread of Angels* (Boston: Cowley Publications, 1997), 16.
7. Matthew 15:16–20.
8. 1 Samuel 13:14.
9. Acts 13:22.

Chapter Four

1. John Claypool, *Tracks of a Fellow Struggler* (New Orleans: Insight Press, 1995), 56–57.

Second Secret: Weak Is the New Strong

1. Philip Yancey, *Disappointment with God* (Grand Rapids, Mich.: Zondervan, 1988).

Chapter Five

1. Henri Nouwen, *Gracias!* (Maryknoll, N.Y.: Orbis Books, 1993), 14–15.
2. 2 Corinthians 12:9–10.

Chapter Six

1. Henri Nouwen, *The Road to Daybreak* (New York: Doubleday, 1988), 118.
2. Christopher de Vinck, *The Power of the Powerless: A Brother's Legacy of Love*, 2nd ed. (Grand Rapids, Mich.: Zondervan, 1995), 14.
3. Henri Nouwen, introduction to *The Power of the Powerless*, by Christopher de Vinck (New York: Doubleday, 1988), xvii-xviii.
4. Daniel 2:1.
5. Daniel 2:47; 3:28–29; 4:34-37.

Chapter Seven

1. Darryl Tippens, *Pilgrim Heart* (Abilene, Tex.: Leafwood Publishers, 2006), 193-94.

Chapter Eight

1. Frederick Buechner, *Listening to Your Life* (New York: HarperOne, 1992), 95.
2. 2 Corinthians 6:10.
3. Philip Yancey, *Rumors of Another World* (Grand Rapids, Mich.: Zondervan, 2003), 197.

Third Secret: Life Together Is Our Only Hope

1. David Wolpe, *Making Loss Matter* (New York: Penguin Putnam, 1999), 35–36.
2. Alister McGrath, *The Journey* (New York: Doubleday, 1999), 149.

Chapter Nine

1. Darryl Tippens, *Pilgrim Heart* (Abilene, Tex.: Leafwood Publishers, 2006), 193-94.
2. John Claypool, *Tracks of a Fellow Struggler* (New Orleans: Insight Press, 1995), 28.
3. These words I spoke to Chris were a paraphrase of a wonderful poem, "Love That Boy," by Walter Dean Myers.

Chapter Ten

1. David Wolpe, *Making Loss Matter* (New York: Penguin Putnam, 1999), 15.
2. Larry Crabb, *The Safest Place on Earth* (Nashville: Word Publishing, 1999), 27.
3. Nicholas Wolterstorff, *Lament for a Son* (Grand Rapids, Mich.: Zondervan, 1987), 92.
4. Annie Dillard, *The Writing Life* (New York: Harper & Row, 1989), 12–13.
5. Galatians 6:17.

Chapter Eleven

1. Nicholas Wolterstorff, *Lament for a Son* (Grand Rapids, Mich.: Zondervan, 1987), 61.
2. Matthew 2:18.

Chapter Twelve

1. Randy Frazee, *The Connecting Church* (Grand Rapids, Mich.: Zondervan, 2001), 242.
2. Henri Nouwen, "The Life of the Beloved," *Thirty Good Minutes,* Program #3502, first aired May 17, 1991.

Chapter Thirteen

1. Anne Lamott, *Traveling Mercies* (New York: Random House, 1999), 74.
2. Rachel Naomi Remen, *My Grandfather's Blessings* (New York: Riverhead Books, 2000), 38.
3. Matthew 2:18.
4. Genesis 35:19–20.
5. Genesis 48:7.
6. Jeremiah 31:15.
7. Greg Boyd, "The Magi and an Arbitrary Massacre," *Christus Victor Ministries* (blog), December 21, 2010, www.gregboyd.org/blog/the-magi-and-an-arbitrary-massacre.
8. Psalm 30:11.

Fourth Secret: The End Is Not the End

1. C. S. Lewis, *The Last Battle* (New York: Macmillan Publishing, 1956), 170–71.

Chapter Fourteen

1. Henri Nouwen *The Path of Waiting* (New York: Crossroads Publishing, 1995), 6.
2. Michael Gorman, *Reading Paul* (Eugene, Ore.: Cascade Books, 2008), 63.
3. John Claypool, *Tracks of a Fellow Struggler* (New Orleans: Insight Press, 1995), 72-73.
4. Henri Nouwen, *The Path of Waiting,* 14–15.
5. Lee Camp, *Mere Discipleship* (Grand Rapids, Mich.: Baker, 2003), 71.
6. Romans 8:35–36.
7. Romans 8:37–39.
8. Romans 8:28.
9. Romans 8:29–30.
10. N. T. Wright, "Commentary on Romans," in *The New Interpreter's Bible* (Nashville: Abingdon, 2002), 10:603.

Chapter Fifteen

1. John Irving, *A Prayer for Owen Meany* (New York: Bloomsbury Publishing, 1989), 251.
2. Larry Crabb, *Inside Out* (Colorado Springs, Colo.: NavPress, 1988), 17-18.
3. Frederick Buechner, *The Sacred Journey* (New York: Harper & Row, 1982), 46.

Chapter Sixteen

1. George Steiner, *Real Presences* (Chicago: University of Chicago Press, 1989), 232.
2. Diane M. Komp, *A Window to Heaven* (Grand Rapids, Mich: Zondervan, 1992), 117–18.
3. Diane M. Komp, *Hope Springs from Mended Places* (Grand Rapids, Mich.: Zondervan, 1994), 75-78.
4. Luke Timothy Johnson, *Living Jesus* (New York: HarperCollins, 1999), 4.
5. 1 Corinthians 11:26.
6. David Wolpe, *Making Loss Matter* (New York: Penguin Putnam, 1999), 22.

Chapter Seventeen

1. Nicholas Wolterstorff, *Lament for a Son* (Grand Rapids, Mich.: Zondervan, 1987), 97.
2. Sharon LaFraniere, "Building a Memorial to a Son, One Child at a Time," *New York Times*, February 5, 2007, www.nytimes.com/2007/02/05/world/africa/05ghana.html.

Chapter Eighteen

1. Frederick Buechner, *The Longing for Home* (New York: HarperCollins, 1996), 140.
2. Pat Conroy, *My Reading Life* (New York: Nan A. Talese, 2010), 187.
3. Retold in Frederick Buechner, *The Longing for Home*, 17.
4. N. T. Wright, *Surprised by Hope* (New York: HarperCollins, 2008), 211.
5. Hebrews 11:13–14.
6. Wendell Berry, "To My Mother," *The Selected Poems of Wendell Berry* (Berkeley, Calif.: Counterpoint Press, 1999).
7. Frederick Buechner, *The Longing for Home*, 28.
8. John O'Donohue, *To Bless the Space between Us* (New York: Doubleday, 2008), 170–71.

Discussion Guide

Introduction

"Everyone who touched [Jesus] was healed" (Mark 6:56).

Do you have a person in your life who has a healing touch?

Who in your life brings healing through their presence, prayer, or touch?

Megan became one of those "little ones" who can't articulate theology but are for us living, breathing icons of Christ's admonition to take no thought for tomorrow, but simply, in faith, to let each day unfold on its own.

How do you become aware of the "little ones" around you, those who can't articulate theology but are for us living, breathing icons of Christ? What have you learned from these "little ones"?

But if you spend your life mourning the fact that you didn't get to Italy, you may never be free to enjoy the very special, the very lovely things . . . about Holland.

What is your "Welcome to Holland" experience?

Chapter 1

"But we have this treasure in jars of clay to show that this all-surpassing power is from God and not from us" (2 Cor. 4:7).

Let the world search for "the perfect egg." But our eyes have been opened by the breaking through of the kingdom in Jesus Christ. We've heard him say, "God bless you—you who are poor in Spirit. God bless you—you who mourn. And God bless you—you who are meek.

How much of your life has been spent hunting for the perfect eggs?

What experiences are opening your eyes to other realities?

Megan's simple-yet-profound life reminded us that God is a heart specialist who looks deeper than accidents of birth.

How has your family background taught you to get ahead in life? More money? Look better? Get into the right university? Tell one more joke? Avoid conflict?

In what ways has your life been built on accidents of birth rather than on the goodness found in your heart?

Chapter 2

The way of David is, from start to finish, a way of imperfection.
—Eugene Peterson

On a scale of 0 to 10, zero being imperfection, even failure, and 10 being perfection, where would you put your life?

Compare that point on the scale with where you expect yourself to be, or where others expect you to be.

The story of finding Israel's second-ever king reminds us again of this first secret that a country spending eight billion dollars annually on cosmetics needs to hear: In a world where people look at the external qualities of a person, God is a heart specialist who values those qualities that have little to do with what a person looks like, how they perform, and how smart they are.

But the LORD said to Samuel, "Do not consider his appearance or his height, for I have rejected him. The LORD does not look at the things human beings look at. People look at the outward appearance, but the LORD looks at the heart" (1 Sam. 16:7).

Reflect on—or share with a group of friends—a time when you were judged by your appearances. What about a time when you judged someone based on appearances?

Barbara Brown Taylor asks, "Was David a good man or a bad man? You decide. I think he was both, as most of us are." (Bread of Angels, 16)

Chapter 3

"Let me win. But if I cannot win, let me be brave in the attempt."— motto of the Special Olympics

Reflect on these life mottos:

"The trouble with the rat race is that even if you win you're still a rat."—Lilly Tomlin

"All the world's a stage and most of us are desperately unrehearsed."—Sean O'Casey

"There are only two tragedies in life: one is not getting what one wants, and the other is getting it."—Oscar Wilde

What is your life motto?

How much do you depend, even thrive, on a daily basis on being judged by others on how you look, how you or your children perform, and how smart you are?

Does this get in the way of God's work on your heart?

Chapter 4

Jesus seems to have told ["prodigal son story"] not primarily for the sake of people like, well, the prodigal son, who know they've failed and need God's grace. Jesus, instead, told the story for those who think they do not need God's grace and who, therefore, worry about associating with people who've blown it.

Are you embarrassed or concerned about associating with people who've blown it?

Do we draw an invisible line between us and people who are divorced, homosexuals, republicans, or democrats?

What are those invisible markers we use to draw those lines? What do we think and do that separates us from people we believe might taint our lives or the lives of our children?

Have you ever been on the receiving end of someone drawing these lines? How did you feel and what have you done about it?

Chapter 5

"But we have this treasure in jars of clay to show that this all-surpassing power is from God and not from us. We are hard pressed on every side, but not crushed; perplexed, but not in despair; persecuted, but not abandoned; struck down, but not destroyed. We always carry around in our body the death of Jesus, so that the life of Jesus may also be revealed in our body. For we who are alive are always being given over to death for Jesus' sake, so that his life may also be revealed in our mortal body. So then, death is at work in us, but life is at work in you" (2 Cor. 4:7-12).

When people rejected Paul's bio, what did he do? What did he say?

"Therefore I will boast all the more gladly about my weaknesses, so that Christ's power may rest on me. That is why, for Christ's sake, I delight in weaknesses, in insults, in hardships, in persecutions, in difficulties" (2 Cor. 12:9-12).

Has your resume ever been rejected?

Tell a story of rejection that helped put your life in perspective? Or perhaps a rejection devastated you. What have you learned from that rejection?

Chapter 6

I'm thankful for all the training I received in languages, in homiletics, in exegesis, in theology, and in practical ministry. But my true teacher was Megan. She was, indeed, a jar of clay. She was broken and frail. Her only full sentence was, "I'm Megan!"

Who are those people around you who are like jars of clay?

What shallowness is exposed in your life by people like this?

The example of the poor widow in Mark 12:41-44 stands in stark contrast to the way Nebuchadnezzar came to know power.

How does your organization, church, school, family get power? Manipulation? Gossip? Secret meetings? Prayer? Bible? Money?

Chapter 7

"In my experience those richest in faith are those who have endured great pain."—Darryl Tippens, *Pilgrim Heart*

Have you made your closest family or friends aware of pain and heartache your carry every day? How did this change your relationship?

If you still carry pain you want to reveal, how could you tell your loved ones? Why should you tell them?

Is there anything you or your friends could learn, ways you could grow by sharing your pain?

What do you learn by seeing others in pain?

After Jesus healed the demon-possessed man, he said, "Go home to your own people and tell them how much the Lord has done for you, and how he has had mercy on you."

Have you ever been healed of a serious physical, spiritual, or mental ailment? What has been your testimony as a result?

Chapter 8

Why would someone make their confession to Megan?

Why would an attorney speak about Megan as his minister?

Why would a missionary point to her as his equipper for ministry?

Why would an old man find such an attachment to her?

Why would a man with so many friends share the deepest secret of his life with this ten year old?

Who would you rather tell your darkest secrets to: Someone who seems to have it all together? Or someone who will look at you with undiluted love?

Read Isaiah 53 and Philippians 2:6-11. In what ways does Christ model the kind of life that we seek?

Chapter 9

Mike wrote the following in his journal in the weeks and months after Megan's death:

I'm a zombie pastor. People think I'm living, but I'm dead. I keep going through the motions of ministry, but inside I'm shell-shocked, numb, lifeless.

I'm in a dark hole. I don't know how deep it is. Or if it gets even deeper. Or if it is ever possible to get out.

I can't breathe. My friends have been my ventilator.

Have you ever had to be literally put on a ventilator in a hospital?

What about emotionally or spiritually—have your friends ever had to intubate you or put you on a ventilator and breath for you when you felt your chest was incapable of taking another breath?

Sometimes our prayers are simply, "Please God" and that's all we can squeeze out of our suffering. Is this why we ask other people to pray for us, or is this "Please, God" prayer enough?

Chapter 10

"We'd much rather be impressively intact than broken. But only broken people share spiritual community."—Larry Crabb

I have a friendship that began just a few years ago with a guy who never knew Megan. When we were getting to know each other, the first thing he said was, "Tell me about Megan. I wish I'd known her." In that request, he was asking to hear my story, willing to look on the scars that her death has left.

But such revealing is difficult for us—we're fearful of what others will think if we reveal our deepest emotional scars. Will they be horrified at such wounds?

Many churches are opening recovery groups of some kind: AA, Celebrate Recovery, Overcomers Anonymous. Reflect on the statement Celebrate Recovery leaders often say, "Celebrate Recovery should not be necessary if the church took this role."

What would happen if we took our friendships deeper by sharing these scars from grief and loss?

Chapter 11

We felt very connected to Matthew's Christmas story, the one that tells of "Rachel weeping for her children" (Matt. 2:17).

As Christmases continue to come around, our family will pass this old tradition along. These quarters remind us that by God's grace we have survived, and that hanging together through joy and sorrow is our only hope of survival.

What are your Christmas traditions?

Do you have any other family traditions that carry you through happy times and sad times?

When grief comes, do you fall into bad habits and leave good traditions behind? Tell about a time when you carried on a tradition, even in a time of grief.

Do you feel connected to Rachel's story of weeping? Do you connect with Megan's story in this book? In what ways?

Chapter 12

The church is not a collection of individuals, but the one body of Christ." —Randy Frazee

Spiritual friendships are critical because they provide the blessing we need in this hurting world to remember that we are loved and valuable—despite our failures and wounds.

How strong are your spiritual friendships that provide comfort and encouragement that you need in your pain?

One evening our little covenant group decided we would bless all the children of our group at the beginning of a school year. Each adult wrote and read a blessing for a child who wasn't their own. All these many years later, and I can still hear the words of Mary as she poured out words of affirmation and love to Megan— thanking her for her simple joy.

Have you ever experienced a time of shared blessings? Consider writing and then reading blessings for your grandchildren, children in your church or home group, a pregnant woman, a family entering a new home, or a family moving away.

Those in pain might end up obsessing about it. But as we move outward in compassion and justice with our friends, neighbors, and strangers, we're invited to move beyond that pain.

How has your pain itself uniquely "qualified" you for deep connections with others?

Chapter 13

Rachel is the Patron Saint of all those who have lost a child, all those who've suffered greatly, all those who think God has forgotten them. But the story is not finally about her alone, of course. This is wonderful, poetic language to say that God has not forgotten.

Do you sometimes feel as if God has forgotten you?

Read the following and discuss:

We live with grief. Life doesn't turn out the way we expect, and we suffer the loss.

The health we expected into old age is suddenly lost.

The child we thought was "normal" turns out to have special challenges.

The teenager we love more than life makes destructive choices.

The job we worked hard for is suddenly lost in a downsized economy.

The marriage we thought was perfect turns out to be wearisome. The one we love so much dies.

Rachel keeps weeping for her children.

Do you hear Rachel's weeping in your family or community?

Chapter 14

Triumphalistic versions of the Christian story seem to forget that we're still living in a world that is "passing away"—one that has yet to be fully re-formed by God through the power of Jesus Christ. The reversal of the curse of Genesis 3 has begun, but it isn't complete.

Do you expect to have most of your prayers answered positively in your favor?

Does your understanding of God cause you to think all the poor will become wealthy? That you will become wealthy if only you have enough faith?

Do you expect that all the sick will be healed if you just believe enough?

These four words—groan, long, wait, and hope—attest to us that something is happening, the salvation story is continuing, the redemption is taking place but it's not here fully, so we should not be surprised when our lives are drenched in seemingly unanswered prayers and tears.

How does being armed with *groaning, longing, waiting, and hoping,* help us not to fall into the pit of despair or try to leap to the peak of final triumph?

Paul affirms that the God who has loved us and called us in Jesus Christ is still here. Familiar with our tears, God has not abandoned or forsaken us.

Read and discuss Romans 8:35-39.

How do these words of Paul impact you—your church and family—today?

Chapter 15

Right now as you are reading this book, you may be experiencing a loss that you've never fully grieved. And this makes me wonder if you've ever fully received the AND YET promises of Jesus.

In what ways have you received the "AND YET" promises of Jesus?

If you could ask God one question about your loss or grief, what would it be?

We had to finally say this: Megan is gone; AND YET we will see her again. The hope of seeing my daughter again is a life-giving breath for me.

Have you ever had to make a resolute statement like this in order to find hope again? What was that statement and how did it restore hope in you?

Chapter 16

"I am the resurrection and the life," said Jesus. Either he is or he isn't. It depends on what happened that weekend in Palestine. For those like me who believe that he was raised by his Father, there is wild hope. Suffering and death do not have the final word. A day is coming when pain, failed relationships, bitterness, depression, and death will be put behind us. Jürgen Moltmann had it right: "God weeps with us so that we may someday laugh with him." That's the outrageous joy called Easter!

"It makes a big difference whether we think someone is dead or alive," Luke Timothy Johnson puts it baldly. "The most important question concerning Jesus, then, is simply this: Do we think he is dead or alive?"

Do you think Jesus is dead or alive?

It is the job of believers to keep reminding one another what time it is. We, like communion, proclaim the Lord's death until he comes.

How are you reminding people around you "what time it is" and that Jesus is alive?

Chapter 17

This chapter is about grief turning into something that a person in the midst of grief could never imagine. As the psalmist says, "You turned my wailing into dancing; you removed my sackcloth and clothed me with joy" (Ps. 30:11).

How is "whistling again" a sign of moving beyond grief, that life wasn't over?

Have you experienced paralyzing grief after the death of a loved one?

What experiences have caused you to want to whistle again?

Jesus had announced in his hometown synagogue that God's Spirit had anointed him to proclaim good news to the poor, to proclaim freedom for the prisoners and recovery of sight for the blind, to set the oppressed free, and to proclaim the year of the Lord's favor (Luke 4:16-30).

Who are the people you have seen today who need to be set free?

Pam and Randy Cope realized as they felt wave-upon-wave of human need that the way of Jesus—even in their brokenness and grief—was sending them into the world in deep need of God's shalom.

What was their response to human trafficking and slavery in particular?

Chapter 18

George Webber, a character in Thomas Wolfe's novel, said, "You can't go back home to your family, back to your childhood . . . back home . . ." Was he right?

What experiences do you have returning to a place you once knew as home?

Did you find the place as you remembered it? Was the feeling satisfying? Sad? Happy? A mix of emotions?

N. T. Wright says of the end times: "To put it bluntly, creation is to be redeemed; that is, space is to be redeemed, time is to be redeemed, and matter is to be redeemed."

The vision of Isaiah 65:17-25 is a new heaven and earth where God will delight in his people and the sound of crying will be no more.

How often does this longing for such a time fill your senses? Seldom? Rarely? Frequently?